HACKING THE VALLEY

HACKING THE VALLEY

An Overview of the Tech Sector, 2014 Edition

ANDREW MEDAL

authorHOUSE®

AuthorHouse™ LLC
1663 Liberty Drive
Bloomington, IN 47403
www.authorhouse.com
Phone: 1-800-839-8640

Published by AuthorHouse 06/23/2014

ISBN: 978-1-4918-9934-2 (sc)
ISBN: 978-1-4918-9933-5 (e)

Library of Congress Control Number: 2014905657

TABLE OF CONTENTS

ACKNOWLEDGEMENTS

To the woman of my dreams—Kimberly Ann. I dedicate this book to you. Our life is so awesome. Love is friendship caught on fire, and ours is so hot ;) It is through you I've learned that being deeply loved by someone gives you strength, while loving someone deeply gives you courage.

I want to thank my Mom for her unconditional support, our friendship and for instilling in me that nerds/geeks rule the world.

I deeply thank my brother Sam, and sisters, Marisa and Aubrey, for being my best friends and for putting up with my incessant rants about life and personal dreams.

I want to thank Jerry for opening my eyes to the tech space through his unadulterated, child-like passion for new electronics, for teaching me the courage to learn and to push the envelope with endless curiosity in seeking solutions.

I thank Matt Dubois, my brother in life, work and play—cheers to our shared goals, visions and dreams. You've been there for me since day one, and I will never forget.

To my Aunt Anita who represents and embodies everything I could ever dream to possess—incorruptible character, unconditional love, integrity, and discipline. I love you. Thank you.

I acknowledge my grandma and grandpa who have taught me the meaning of true family. Grandpa, your success made me want to be a businessman, and shaped my life. Gram, you are the warmest, most joy-filled person I've ever met, and the definition of a the perfect grandma.

Danielle, Dave, Matt, Rachel, Hannah, Leah and Tristan, I love guys and am so grateful we are all family.

Jason, I look forward to building a personal and business relationship, you are an inspiration and motivation.

Thank you to all of my aunts, uncles and cousins. Uncle Mark, without my experience at Nema/Toolshed I don't know if I would have ever understood the value of a true salesman. My time there helped me realize my entrepreneurial destiny quicker. Thank you for giving me the opportunity to learn when I was younger. Aunt Steph and Uncle R. Thanks for simply giving me a job when I needed it—the warehouse was a necessary means to an end. I love you both.

My crew from way back when who will always be a part of my life through all the ups and downs—DC, Crenshaw, Pizi, Atkinson, Chuck, Rich, Kibbee, Rookie and Pants.

To my dad, who taught me how to be uniquely confident and loving, from afar, I wish you all the best.

Deep appreciation and respect goes out to all of the heroes I covered in my writing. Without your courage and foresight to go where there is no path, none of us would have the chance to follow your trail. Also very special thanks to the tech history scribes, who without your journalistic gifts and talents, none of us would ever comprehend or realize the magic taking place around us—Especially Ashlee Vance and Steven Levy who reaffirm the 80:20 rule, you both inspire and motivate me to no end.

Thanks to God for showing me the silver lining in all my trials. I give praise to Him in all I do, with constant thanksgiving and petition in prayer. It is with Your Favor and Grace all things are possible.

AUTHOR'S NOTE

I am an entrepreneur.

In April 2011, I picked up a one year old issue of Inc. Magazine from March 2010. Something funny then occurred that piqued my interest. I noticed that the "coming trends" and the "what to look for in the future" type articles, from that older issue, were in fact relevant trends and the startups getting most buzz at this moment in time (April, 2011). We all know that technology is constantly evolving, and what was relevant today can be outdated tomorrow. It made me wonder and think, "What is the speed in which today's technology trends and hot startup ideas could be irrelevant tomorrow?"

This question became the thesis of my writing. I started collecting articles from a number of different sources and gathering information about the noticeable people, companies and trends in the tech sector to create a somewhat thorough snapshot of the space during a given point in time. That given point in time spanned over two years through April 2011 to April 2013.

My hope is that anyone who reads my findings can learn a great deal about the tech space during that period, identify any overlap between people, trends and business topics, and if they so desire I hope my research helps to give insight into what type of future trends to expect in the short to mid-term.

Most of my writing is a summation of each individual article (with credit given to each article, author and proper citation) that I encountered in my research, which is where the chapters find their origin.

As for the topics, trends and people, obviously since my writing, there will have been updates whether good, bad or indifferent to each. Meaning that the information I provide in this book and research may not be the most updated news per each topic. My research is simply a snapshot in that period of time. However, while reading my research, you may find little facts that show progress on a particular topic. For instance, Facebook comes to mind, early in the book with a chapter in 2011 one in eight people had a FB account, then later in the book towards 2012-2013, FB had amassed their billionth user changing their numbers to

1 in 7 people on the planet. If you pay attention, you will catch little facts like that throughout the book.

In this digital age of data, it is commonplace to get inundated by information with an infinite and always growing number of social media sites bombarding us with second-by-second chatter, dogmatic blog posts, daily e-mail newsletters and subscriptions, mass texts and e-mails. It has been said that getting information from the Internet is like getting a drink of water from a fire hydrant. It is nearly impossible to cut through the rubbish and find the cherished information. Even coveted sources sometimes lose their appeal when taken over by the mainstream.

I chose to return to more traditional sources, in an effort to keep my findings more pure, concise and less flawed. It is somewhat ironic that I used more traditional print materials, than digital, to write a book about tech. My daily research came through the Wall Street Journal and San Jose Mercury (my preferred source of Silicon Valley news) newspapers; my weekly information came from Bloomberg BusinessWeek, which I believe does a real good job of focusing on facts and numbers versus opinions while my monthly and quarterly data came from my numerous magazine sources.

INTRO

For the past two years, I've been extensively researching the tech sector. My research includes: Key figures within the sector, industry trends, prominent news and innovative applications. The following information is presented chronologically as I encountered it through the dates of April 2011 to April 2013. The goal for my exploration was to understand current trends, position myself to better predict future trends, and most importantly to satisfy my passion for technology. During my investigation, I utilized numerous sources;

- The Wall Street Journal
- The San Jose Mercury Newspaper (Silicon Valley's Preeminent Paper)
- Wired Magazine
- Entrepreneur Magazine
- Fast Company
- Inc.
- Bloomberg Business Week
- Numerous Industry Insider Blogs (Notably Ben Horowitz, Marc Andreesen, Paul Graham & Mark Suster)
- Forbes
- Fortune
- Newsbeast

An inescapable collision occurred due to my immersion in the sector and my innate entrepreneurial spirit. This event led to the birth of a multitude of unique and disruptive business concepts. I took great pleasure in "hacking" the industry for the past two years. I hope you delight in my findings; this book is the cultivation of my journey.

Each chapter was constructed by the various sources I listed and the articles that struck me as "relevant at the time," which best support the goal of my writing. Each article led to the design of that particular chapter.

YURI MILNER: THE RISE OF THE RUSSIAN

Yuri Milner is said to be the world's most successful investor in social media. Milner, self-made billionaire has literally bought his way into the most recognizable, promising, young, technology companies, while ruthlessly disrupting the traditional venture capital model. Like a thief in the night, his fund has gone from zero equity to more than $12 billion in assets.

Starting with his $200 million midnight infusion in Facebook in 2009 and establishing major positions in Zynga, Groupon, Twitter and Spotify—his mystique is as much a boon as it is a hindrance. One of the early backers of his investment firm, Digital Sky Technologies is Alisher Usmanov—one of the richest billionaires in all of Russia. Usmanov's background includes accusations of Kremlin associations and an overturned conviction for fraud and extortion. He has an approximate $18 billion war chest in mining, steel and Telecom, as well as ownership stake in a British football team.

With Yuri at its helm, Digital Sky Technologies plays the venture capital game unlike anyone has ever seen. His three secretaries rotate on 8-hour shifts. DST is open 24 hours a day and is constantly traveling. Yuri is a thesis investor and knows the kinds of companies he wants and buys on trends. "Other VC firms say they're thesis investors but they're not and get nervous on every deal," says Eric Lefkofsy, cofounder of Groupon.

He researches a company for at least a year before investing and acts on 10 to 20 different factors. He says, "You can't write a formula, it's partially science, partially art."

His investments are founder favorable; He never takes a board seat, is willing to invest in additional rounds, and only gets involved in decision making when approached by the founder. His approach has earned him a strong reputation within founder circles.

His takeover of Silicon Valley was seemingly predestined. After the fall of The Soviet Union, a class of robber barons—the oligarchs—rose to control much of Russia's abundant resources. In a disorganized and corrupt process of privatization, Russia's export wealth switched from government to private hands.

Not coincidentally enough, most of the oligarchs were Jewish. During the Soviet Union, Jews thrived in the gray and black markets, and were the earliest capitalists in Russia when capitalism arose. Milner himself was a hustler in the gray markets at the end of the Soviet

Union. He bought old DOS machines, which were imported or smuggled from the U.S., and made the drop at directed street points. His father, Boris Milner, an 81-year old former professor—in American management nonetheless—was not happy with his son's career path and urged him to focus back on his studies. At that time, he was a physics graduate student, and partly due to his ambition and his father's desire, decided to pursue an American MBA. In 1990 Yuri enrolled at the University of Pennsylvania's Wharton School. Wharton introduced him to a new culture (he actually showed up in a suit and tie at his first class, the way they did in Russia), and a new way of doing business. The early 90's was the era of the hostile takeover expert—Henry Kravis, Carl Icahn and Michael Milken. Milner fell in love with their style and studied their every move.

From Wharton he spent three years in Washington, D.C. at the World Bank's financial sector branch. He watched the privatization of Russia from a distance and saw individuals with the right connections secure their bank as oligarchs (including Usmanov). While working at the World Bank, he met the right people and made powerful connections. After just a few meetings, Mikhail Khodorkovsky, the now imprisoned oil baron and public Putin enemy, appointed Yuri head of his investment brokerage house. Milner convinced Khodorkovsky to allow him to quarterback the first hostile takeover of a public company in post-Soviet times, a Russian candy company. The takeover failed though, however, and Yuri decided to venture out on his own. Despite the failed takeover, during the initiative, he had met Gregory Finger who ran the Russian office of the U.S. hedge fund, New Century Holdings. At that time, New Century was one of the biggest purchasers of Russian securities. In 1999, Milner saw the Russian online opportunity as being ripe for investment and persuaded Finger and New Century Holdings to co-invest into a venture fund. New Century agreed to place $2.25 million if Finger and Milner pledged $750K of their own cash. The year before, Yuri had assembled a group of investors to purchase a macaroni factory. Russia had just defaulted on their debt and he knew it meant the end of imported macaroni. And, so, he parlayed his factory profits into the venture fund.

The fund, dubbed NetBridge, sought any tech company that mirrored large online companies in the U.S. The firm made some minor investments but ran into obstacles amidst the bursting of the Dot-Com bubble. Yet, Milner, being the opportunistic predator he is, made the best of the downturn and induced the admired online portal Port.Ru to merge with his NetBridge. Little did anyone know, especially the elites of Silicon Valley that this was the beginning of an online empire even the most successful oligarch would envy.

By 2005, Mail.Ru had solidified its dominance in the Russian internet and was ready to flex its innovation muscle. The company tested virtual credits and online gaming before Zynga and Facebook. In 2007, Mail.Ru released e-mail paired with instant messaging, a whole year before Facebook released its chat function.

The same year, the economy had made a turnaround and Yuri was ready to raise new funds. He created Digital Sky Technologies as an investment holding company and was ready to target the Russian web. However, by that time, Russia was starting to be seen as a safe place for foreign investors, and he decided to open DST to new outsiders. New York hedge fund Tiger Global, Goldman and Renaissance Capital all made investments, all who were primarily interested in the growth potential of Mail.Ru, which made up about two-thirds of Digital Sky's portfolio.

In 2008, Milner wanted to buy into Facebook and at the peak of the global financial crisis was bold enough to raise a second fund—Digital Sky Technologies Global.

Milner was put in touch with Usmanov, who was then looking to place capital in the Russian internet. "I found Mr. Milner's vision of the Internet's future and the way he developed his business appealing," says Usmanov. He invested $350 million into Mail.Ru and agreed to capitalize DST Global in late 2008 (roughly $1 billion).

Since his blitzkrieg $200 million investment into Facebook, for a 2 percent equity stake, he has since invested $125 million more. In two years, DST Global took up big positions in the Internet's most attractive budding companies:

- FB $200 million; May 2009
- Zynga $180 million; December 2009
- Groupon $135 million; April 2010
- FB $125 million; January 2011
- Spotify $100 million; June 2011
- Airbnb $112 million; July 2011
- Twitter $400 million; July 2011

With his industry altering style of investment, astute vision for the future of the Internet and "bottomless pockets," he has not only bought himself a ticket to the most exclusive party on the planet, he has become a main host. He's already turned the late-stage venture funding on its head and is now rewriting the rules of seed funding. In January 2011, committing only personal funds alongside super-angel investor Ron Conway, Milner advanced $150K convertible debt to every single one of the 43 startups nurtured by Y Combinator in its last batch. Milner states that Paul Graham, cofounder of Y Combinator, is one of his heroes.

Graham obviously sees value in Milner because since DST Global lent that initial convertible debt, the arrangement has been made permanent to the Y Combinator program.

Paul Graham and the Valley are not the only ones who've taken heed to Milner's effortless artistry. In 2011, Milner was invited to be one of six technology figures that reads like a who's who of the industry to brief the G8 nations in that year's summit. He delivered a cunning message about social technology and how he views social networks as steps in the creation of a global brain. He feels the social landscape, in its entirety, adds up to a new collaborative consciousness that transforms the very nature of information and the existing monopolies who supply it.

In the blink of an eye, Yuri Milner has shifted the balance of decades-old technology money, but has also updated the power spectrum. Not only is he now connected, in some way, to every major player in the technology sector, including Y Combinator's Paul Graham, super-angel Ron Conway, Zuckerberg, Groupon's Andrew Mason—he is arguably more important. The street-corner hustler turned technology tycoon has amassed wealth, prestige and power even the first generation oligarchs would envy. And did this all by the way, without graduating from Wharton—he was, in fact, a few credits short.

Forbes, March 2011, The Billionaire Who Friended the Web. Parmy Olson,
Wired Magazine, November 2011, The Outsider. Michael Wolff

KEVIN RYAN: A BILLIONAIRE'S GILT

"In some ways, we're like China [referring to Silicon Valley] and Silicon Valley is like the U.S. Yes, they still are much bigger, but we're growing much faster," says Kevin Ryan. Ryan is the billion-dollar man of New York's tech hub, Silicon Alley, leading the charge. He sold double click, an online advertising company, for more than $1 billion, is founder and CEO of Gilt Groupe, the fashion flash-sale site, which is valued over $1 billion, and is cofounder and chairman of 10gen, which develops open source databases that is worth another $1 billion. Additionally, Ryan was an early backer in Hot Jobs (sold for a petty $450 million) and is the founder and chairman of Business Insider, a financial-news-aggregation site that has an extremely bright future.

In the November 2011 issue of the Wall Street Journal Magazine, Adrienne Gaffney breaks down a day in the life of Kevin Ryan. As Gaffney tells us in the article, "Ryan's weekday is a careful balance between personal health, family and work. His day is scheduled virtually down to the minute."

He starts his day at 6:15am and heads to the Reebok Sports Club on the Upper West Side. By 7:15am he's back at home for breakfast with his kids. At 8:30am he heads to Park Avenue, where the Gilt Groupe offices are located, before most other employees. At that time, Gilt Groupe had 850 employees. Ryan interviews applicants nearly every single day and does all the hiring. Any unscheduled time in his day is spent responding to e-mails, typically no more than 30 minutes a day, and on average he will receive 200 e-mails while responding to 40. 90% of his time is devoted to working on Gilt, while Business Insider and 10gen receive 5% each. Under the Gilt umbrella are seven sites: Gilt, Gilt Home, Gilt Man, Gilt City, Gilt Taste, Park & Bond, and Jetsetter. No matter the billions his companies are valued at, he always makes time for his health and family which leaves him living Gilt free.

Wall Street Journal Magazine, November 2011, Silicon Valley Insider, Adrienne Gaffney

JEFF BEZOS:
THE INTERNET'S CHIEF DISRUPTOR

In September 2011, Amazon shook up the tablet market by releasing its first Amazon tablet—named the Kindle Fire. The Kindle was not just an assault on the tablet market and its primary market shareholder (Apple's iPad), but an attack on the core vision of how Apple approached the space and its underlying foundational beliefs.

Breaking the status-quo chains is nothing new for Jeff Bezos, who has been driving Amazon's disruption vehicle for the past 15 years. Amazon's approach to the tablet market by offering premium products at non-premium prices (at the time Kindle Fire starts at $199 versus Apple's iPad at $499) is merely scratching the surface. In Wired Magazine's December, 2011 interview with Jeff Bezos, he sees the Fire as a "media service" rather than a device, as opposed to Apple which sees their iPad as a flagship product in the post-PC era, where desktop is replaced by light, portable tablets. The bottom-line differences between the two companies, starts exactly there; Apple is primarily a hardware company and delivers 91 percent of its revenues from its coveted devices, with iTunes contributing a 6 percent sliver. The focus on product design, marketing and special product launches all show the significance Apple places on the device itself. Amazon, on the other side, is content centered with roughly 50 percent of its sales generated from media like books, TV shows, music and movies. The iPad underscores downloads (think movies, music, TV shows—all media) and makes users save everything to their devices in order to use the media. The industry refers to the "downloading to machine process" as local storage. In order for a user to save a lot of media, he or she must have a device with a large memory, thus putting a premium on devices with larger memories. By comparison, Amazon focuses on streaming. Fire users are able to store up to 20 GB of music at no cost on Amazon's servers and an unlimited amount of music that users purchase directly from Amazon, which is then streamed freely. Plus, users can stream more than 100,000 videos for free. In other words, the iPad is device-centric and the Fire is cloud-centric. Through the Kindle Fire, Amazon is giving the public an entirely new alternative to computing to Apple's post-PC approach, Amazon is taking the post-web strategy. A case in point, Apple emphasizes owning and developing their own operating system (Apple iOS) while Amazon simply outsources it to Google's Android. Apple believes in specialized apps, while Amazon believes in a specialized browser. Apple sees hardware as king, Amazon sees content.

This disrupting nature can be traced back to Bezos' vision for the future and the culture he's nurtured in Amazon. Talking about Amazon's culture he says, "As a company, we are culturally pioneers, and we like to disrupt even our own business. Other companies have different cultures and sometimes don't like to do that. Our job is to bring those industries along."

And that is exactly what Bezos and Amazon have done. At the date of the Wired article being published, Amazon had stealthily captured market share in each consumer content segment, with a major footprint in each medium. 60 percent in the book marketplace, 22 percent in video, 19 percent in music, 19 percent in consumer electronics and its web service division had retained one-fifth of the cloud computing market at 19 percent market share.

What began as a way for Amazon's computer engineers to work together efficiently has become a multi-billion dollar powerhouse division. Speaking of cloud computing space, one observer has said that Amazon is the Coke of the field, and there's no Pepsi. Amazon Web Services host some of the most admired sites on the web, and is accountable for an impressive amount of the world's online traffic. For instance, Foursquare relies on Amazon's cloud computing platform with 3 million check-ins a day, Harvard medical school utilizes its services for an expansive database that develops genome-analysis models, the NASA jet propulsion lab processes Hi-Res satellite images to guide its robots, Netflix's video streaming service hosts with AWS (Amazon Web Services) and accounts for 25 percent of U.S. internet traffic, Newsweek/The Daily Beast have 1 million page views every hour through AWS, the U.S. Department of Agriculture which houses a geographic information system for food-stamp recipients, Virgin Atlantic has a crowdsourced travel review service and even Yelp stores 22 million-plus reviews on Amazon's cloud hosting servers.

The success behind Amazon's Web Service Division, its dominance in the E-commerce sector and every other industry Amazon chooses to enter is a direct reflection of Jeff Bezos' stick-to-itiveness in business. As he says, "At Amazon, we like things to work in five to seven years. We're willing to plant seeds, let them grow—and we're very stubborn. We say we're stubborn on vision and flexible on details." Since its inception, with Bezos as its guiding light, Amazon has disrupted our daily lives—it changed the way we do everyday shopping, how we read and purchase books, how we engage with all types of content and even how the Internet itself is powered. So, what's next? Well, with Jeff's next project—Blue Origin—he'd like to make it so anybody can go into space. He's looking to increase the safety and decrease the cost. With his track record of disruption success, I don't doubt whatsoever that he'll be able to accomplish his mission. And just maybe Blue Origin will showcase just how out-of-this-world Jeff Bezos' forward thinking has been, further substantiating that he may be the premier technologist of the post-web era.

Wired Magazine, December, 2011, CEO of the Internet. Steven Levy

STEVE JOBS: A TRIBUTE TO THE ICON

Wired is my absolute favorite magazine because somehow, in each article published, they are able to capture and bottle up in words, the magic and mystique that constitute the tech industry. Their December 2011 tribute article to Steve Jobs by Steven Levy is no different.

At the date of the article, 28 years prior, in November 1983, Steven Levy met Jobs and had his first interview with the icon. The reason for the article was the release of the Macintosh, which Apple was preparing to launch. During the interview Levy asked Jobs if he feared the consequences assuming the Mac bombed, like the Apple III had. "Yeah," he had admitted. "But, God if you are not willing to get out there and do it again, what's the point? I'm not doing this for the money. I never have. I have more money than I can ever give away in a lifetime. I'm doing it because I love it. If it falls on its face and it's another failure, I should write poetry or something, go climb a mountain."

Even back then, at 28 years old, Steve Jobs spoke about Apple as he would repeatedly in the future, as "an intersection between science and aesthetics."

Referring to the Apple logo and then life in general, he said, "Simplicity is the ultimate sophistication. When you start looking at a problem, it seems really simple—because you don't understand its complexity, and your solutions are way too oversimplified, and they don't work. Then you get into the problem and you see it's really complicated. And you come up with all of these solutions. That's where most people stop, and the solutions tend to work for a while. But the really great person will keep going and find the key underlying principle of the problem and sort of come full circle with a beautiful elegant solution that works. And that's what we wanted to do with the Mac."

So what happened? Despite great hype and a fanatic cult of followers, the Mac sold well below projections. And, in 1985, the company Jobs created, exiled him from its ranks.

For the next 12 years (from 1985 to 1997) Jobs roamed the business desert, referring back to the time period as his "wilderness years."

In his "wilderness years" Jobs started the next computer company and acquired Pixar Studios from George Lucas. Here is what George Lucas said about Jobs during these years: "Steve Jobs had a vision. He believed in something that no one could see, and he followed that path wherever it led him, against all odds and against all doubters. Along the way he had real hurdles to overcome and real drama. At NeXT, Steve was in a sort of purgatory. I don't think NeXT was his primary vision—it was just what he could do at the time. He bought Pixar from me around then, too, but I think Pixar was just something that fascinated him— not something that drove him. Eventually the drought and famine descended upon Apple and they called him back. That's when his story really became the hero's journey. He returned and reinstituted his vision."

And that is exactly what he did. In 1997, Jobs was implored to return to Apple as interim CEO. Speaking about the Apple he returned to, he said, "The company needs to spend a lot of time in the gym getting back in shape, and maybe I can play a small role as the trainer. Even though I'm a swimmer and runner, what I do is team sports. It took a lot of people to build the Mac, to build Apple. I think to these people I'm a symbol or the spirit of the Apple they love."

The reason Jobs said he wanted to return to Apple was that, "I decided that the world is a slightly better place with Apple in it. I've worked really hard since I was 20 years old. I'm now in my forties and am going to do the best I can here. And I'm doing it for me, for some things I have in my heart about the company."

Job's vision for the future of Apple was simple. He would lean down its overweight product line to one high-quality product in four separate categories. That would become Apple's core offerings and where he would have the teams focus their efforts. Again, referring to the Apple he went back to, he said Apple was now a textbook example of the kind of soulless company he'd hoped it would never become. It seemed to suggest that growth inevitably brings compromise. "But I've never delivered that in my whole life— never, ever," he said.

By 2000, he had dropped the "interim" from his CEO title and had returned to his God destined position. Meanwhile, Jobs' keynote speeches, where he would unveil Apple's new products, had become the most sought after show in technology. His own excitement and satisfaction with his products shone through, and his natural ability to present his products with an element of surprise left the world wanting more. He knew the importance of secrets, and at every "show" would unveil his products without any of the public knowing exactly what to expect. He did it first in 1984 with the original Mac, in 1999 with the iBook, he did it with the iMac, with iTunes, iPods, the iPad, with software, with software updates. And every presentation was always as exciting as the one before, and the one to come. In fact, his presentations became his signature moments—the ones that have defined his legacy and captured his brilliance. Him up on stage, a black mock turtle neck, blue jeans, wire frame glasses, Apple logo radiating behind him—this is how the world has come to know the great, legendary, Steve Jobs.

On October 2011, Jobs left the stage for good. And the world lost a hero. Jobs used to say, "If today were the last day of my life, would I want to do what I am about to do today?" If the answer is no for too many days in a row, he said, "It's time to make a change." Early in his life, at 28, Jobs' mission for Apple was for it to become a $10 billion company and not lose its soul. His $10 billion aim paled in comparison to the success Apple has encountered—holding the title of the most valuable company on the planet more than once. Steve Jobs died a hero, and became a legend and, although he is no longer with us in person, his soul lives through Apple, giving it life and character, like only the great Steve Jobs could.

Wired Magazine, December 2011, The Revolution According to Steve Jobs. Steven Levy

BILL GATES AND WARREN BUFFET: THE BILLIONAIRE PLEDGE, THE WORLD'S MOST PRESTIGIOUS CLUB

"One way or another, we form ideas about what we're going to do if we turn out to be wealthy. For me it was in my 20's, reading what those other people had done," Warren Buffet says. "Those other people" Buffet is referring to are the great American business tycoons—from Andrew Carnegie to J.P. Morgan to John D. Rockefeller to his son John Rockefeller Jr. of course, his initial attraction was by their artistry to stockpile mass amounts of cash. But he was also impressed by the way the titans turned philanthropists late in their careers. The Rockefellers used their fortune to start the green revolution in global agriculture, cure disease and fund countless arts and cultural programs.

In the December 2011 issue of The Wall Street Journal Magazine, Robert Frank wrote a piece highlighting Buffet and Gates' Giving Pledge which they launched in 2010. The pledge itself is simple in its requirements: the signers must be billionaires and they have to give at least half of their fortune to charity during their lifetime. Their mission is to inspire the world's wealthy to give a larger percentage of their accumulated fortune to charity. At the time of the publication of the article, sixty nine billionaires had signed the pledge representing more than $150 billion in charitable donations.

Buffet says that many of the givers were already committed to giving a portion of their fortune away but were inspired to promise a specific number. Others decided to give their first donation ever. Facebook billionaire Mark Zuckerberg, a pledge signer, states, "People wait until late in their career to give back but why wait when there is so much to be done?" Another pledge signer, 55-year old billionaire founder of Morningstar (the Chicago-based investment research company) Joe Mansueto says, "I'm so focused on building Morningstar that I figured philanthropy would come later in life. Then one afternoon in August 2010, I received a phone call from Buffet explaining that if enough people sign the Pledge, we could really have an effect on giving in our society over time. Both Buffet and Gates have inspired me and set this example to the world of the responsible way to have wealth. The Giving Pledge sends a message to those with wealth to think beyond their own narrow interests to the greater needs of society."

I think a lot of people are coming out of the woodwork and saying, "Now we're going to give." People are now talking about philanthropy like they never did before, and the Pledge had a lot to do with that," Ron Perelman, the New York billionaire, financier, and Pledge signer claims.

One billionaire who was lured into the cause was John Paul DeJoria, the "shampoo billionaire" who co-founded the Paul Mitchell Empire, acknowledges that he and Buffett are very different people. DeJoria grew up homeless on the streets of L.A. prior to becoming a hair product tycoon and also the man behind Patron Tequila. He sports his hair in a ponytail, collects mansions and wears black. Yet, they hit it off when it came to giving back. "Warren said, 'Join our club,' and I said, 'Where do I sign?'" DeJoria recalls.

Through their joint venture, Buffett and Gates have taken philanthropy to new heights and sparked a radical change in the world of philanthropy. Buffett says. "The true success of the Pledge will be revealed over time, when a future Warren Buffett reads about their efforts and decides to follow in their footsteps."

Wall Street Journal Magazine, December 2011, The Biggest Gift in the World. Robert Frank

BECOMING A MULTI-BILLIONAIRE: ONE THOUSAND MILLIONS AT A TIME

In the March 2011 issue of Forbes, Rich Karlgaard talks about how to become a billionaire zero by zero. He states, "Fact is, it's darn hard to land on the Forbes' billionaire list. Staring your own company is still the best path to becoming a billionaire, but the hill steepens for each additional zero of net worth."

An eight-figure net worth—$10 million to $99 million—constitutes millionaire status but is two zeroes short of being billionaire. Every city of size in the U.S. has dozens or hundreds of these types. They can be partners of big city law firms or top investment banks, owners of franchises that spit out nice cash flows, real estate investors, small business owners or CEOs of publicly traded companies.

The probability decreases when we add another zero to nine figures—$100 million to $999 million—still one zero shy of billionaire rank. The quickest way to obtain this wealth is to start a company that the markets love, and be acquired by a larger company with a high market cap and a war chest of cash.

Well then, how does one become a billionaire? Karlgaard says, "Outside of Wall Street the best way is to start a company that rides the Moore's law curve and scales globally." Bill Gates can attest to that—in 2011 (the year Karlgaard published his article), Gates was the second richest man in the world with $56 billion although, had he not given away $30 billion with his pal Buffett in their Giving Pledge, he would've had the top spot. And Microsoft in its heyday was a prime example of a company surfing Moore's law curve.

In fact, Intel's CEO Paul Otellini states that Moore's law was assured for another five years and computing will be eight times more powerful than today's prices. In other words, one dollar of today's computing power will cost 3 cents five years from now.

What will the future look like then? What new applications, mobile breakthroughs and super-computing capabilities will arise? How will technology change our daily lives? If you can answer those questions, you'll solidify yourself a spot on the future Forbes billionaire list—just like Gates.

Forbes, March 2011, How to Become a Billionaire Zero by Zero. Rich Karlgaard
Forbes, March 2011, The Billionaire's List Issue. Steven Bertoni

WELCOME TO THE FUTURE: ENTREPRENEURS INVENTING IT THE WAY THEY ENVISION

Steve Jobs said that the best way to predict the future is to invent it. Welcome to the future—supercomputers that fit in the palm of your hand, cars that drive you, solar power—from space, commercial flights to the moon. Future-innovators, not referring to the next generation of creative minds, but talking about those individuals who bend the future to their personal visions of how it will be, individuals like Jobs, Elon Musk and Sir Richard Branson are all making it possible.

In January 2012, Fortune published their "Guide to the Future," after consulting with dozens of researchers, forecasters, security experts and analysts. Experts provided a mostly optimistic view based on scientific and technological breakthroughs that will improve our daily lives.

They claim business leaders will need to adjust to a democratization of the workplace, hierarchies may disappear and teams may function without leaders. Future CEOs will have to manage a complex business of inputs emitted from billions of phones, sensors and other connecting machines. Companies that can manage and mine all those bits and bytes will effortlessly ride the Moore's Law curve to sector dominance.

Forecasters envision a high-tech workplace with disruptive technologies such as the Hologram Table which uses special lenses and lights to project 3D holograms of real world objects. Smart Glass which can morph from solar panel to multi-media screen, to frosted privacy shade. Insta-Manufacturing is an affordable desktop-size 3D printer that will allow employees to produce small prototypes. Talking With Your Hands is the same technology that powers consoles like Microsoft Kinect, which enables users to navigate computer screens with a flick of the wrist.

According to Forbes, many of the impactful changes to the way we work will be unapparent to the eye. Smart phones will be as powerful as mainframes allowing heavy computing on the go. Phones will be loaded with all kinds of office basics like your health insurance card, your digital wallet and software that will track employee whereabouts that will support employee collaboration.

Of course, this assumes anyone will be going to the office in the future. Futurists anticipate the end of a central office, replaced by contractors and telecommuters operating via satellite location.

Fortune, January 2012, Fortune's Guide to the Future. Nina Easton

THE FUTURE OF NOW: TODAY'S INNOVATORS SOLVING TOMORROW'S PROBLEMS

Today's entrepreneurs have the opportunity to solve puzzles never faced before in history. A growing world population, increasing resource consumption and technological advancements have all contributed to creating extraordinary wicked problems. These wicked problems have been created by the multiplying use of all-electric vehicles worldwide and an expected world energy demand boom forcing the need for alternative energy sources.

In 2012, the world's total sales for all-electric vehicles were a little less than 25,000 cars. By 2017, projected annual sales are expected to sky rocket to roughly a million vehicles. That's all fine and dandy for the environment except one caveat—range anxiety—the very real fear of running out of battery power in the middle of nowhere. Today's electronics have a battery range of an average 100 miles. However, with scientific breakthroughs, IBM and some 50 other cars are working on battery enhancements that would allow 500 miles a charge. The core battery technology is referred to as lithium-air and was invented in the 1990's by scientists who deducted that they could create energy by combining lithium with oxygen. This new battery technology is looking to completely replace traditional lithium-ion power packs. The lithium-ion batteries are sealed, which requires a large and heavy metal cathode to conduct the electric current. Lithium-air batteries use oxygen in the air eliminating the need for the cathode, which results in a battery with a 500 mile range. Range is not the only issue—recharging any battery presents an issue, as well as durability and forcing the battery to release power quickly enough mandates costly nanotechnology. However, in the face of these types of massive obstacles, true visionaries and innovators thrive best and IBM's lead researcher sees a lithium-air prototype by the end of 2013 and commercialization by decade's end.

Three bold ideas have emerged in order to combat the world's expected energy boom which, in 2012, had oil demand at the 12 to 15 billion "oil equivalent" levels, and by 2035 "oil equivalent" levels are expected to rise between 17 to 20 billion annual tons. The first—harnessing the sun's power, is not new, but the approach is. The second idea is creating electricity in space and lastly, tapping fuel from the ocean floor.

With the idea of cold fusion failing pathetically, scientists went back to the drawing board for a new approach to controlling the sun's energy. This resulted in two forward-thinking reactor designs, which are currently being explored by the research world. One is called a *tokamak* and the other is an inertial confinement system, and although they are 20 to 30 years off, show promise. The issue is that both designs demand either colossal superconducting magnetic forces or extra-fierce laser arrays and projected to cost tens of billions. General Fusion, a small Canadian company, has developed a possibly even more effective technology called magnetized target fusion, which would cost a fraction of what the other designs do. Doug Richmond, General Fusion's CEO, says the company is promising to demonstrate a net energy gain in five years and meeting their milestones. This has been accomplished in part by its private funding, which has attracted $32 million from investors including Amazon CEO Jeff Bezos. General Fusion's design is similar to the other two designs, but plans to use simpler and less expensive hardware. The company has been successful in past projects with the U.S. Navy and if it is successful in its current endeavor will provide safe, clean energy to support the world's coming energy boom.

Another out of this world idea that could someday soon come to fruition is beaming solar power down to earth from space. The process starts with panels orbiting in space—free from clouds, rain and nighttime—gathering solar energy 24/7. The panel's photovoltaic cells capture sunlight and convert it into energy and then the energy is sent to earth in the form of a high-power microwave beam. A ground receiver then catches the energy from the beam, turns it into electricity and sends it to the power grid. The hang-up is cost—building a space solar system would require billions in capital outlay. Fortunately, with ventures like Microsoft cofounder Paul Allen's aircraft, which would offer an affordable way to launch satellites, and the fact that solar panels are getting less expensive, are making this process much more feasible than so pie-in-the-sky.

Another surprising source of energy/biofuel researchers are now exploring is seaweed. There are a multitude of reasons why it could become a valuable source—it's one of the fastest growing plants, doesn't need fertilizer, demands less space than land-based crops and its fuel emits less CO_2 than corn (the current ethanol champion). The unknown variable is whether or not the technology can scale affordably. Assuming it can, it would empower the world with a fuel that is cheaper than alternatives.

In a race to solve tomorrow's wicked problems today, scientists and entrepreneurs are making huge strides. With audacious visions and courageous innovators all the aforementioned technologies are quickly becoming more science than fiction.

Fortune, New Ways to Solve the Energy Problem, January, 2012. Stuart Brown & Anne VanderMey

RON CONWAY: SUPER ANGEL BY DAY, BOSS OF THE RONTOURAGE BY NIGHT

Ron Conway could possibly be the coolest dude on the planet. Don't take my word for it; ask all the entrepreneurs he's invested in. As Miguel Helft's February 2012 Fortune article informs us, shortly after being inducted into the Conway clique, the entrepreneurs receive a spreadsheet. It's dubbed the SV Angel (his investment firm) "partner list." In miniature font, the list expands to 18 pages and embodies more than 1,300 treasured business connections. A Conway investment comes with the covenant of an introduction to anyone on the list. The "partner list" has an electrifying effect for those initiated into Conway's crew. Most investors make introductions for their companies, obviously they have vested interest, but that's not the point. What makes Conway so potent is: 1. the quality of his connections and 2. the fact that he's always on. He has no hobbies other than philanthropy, and his social life orbits around the Valley's conferences, charity events and socialite parties. The events are simply an opening to flex his powerful Rolodex muscle.

What an impressive Rolodex he's amassed. It is widely recognized as the most coveted Rolodex in Silicon Valley. The list encompasses every corner of the tech world, from professional investors, to attorneys, top media/journalist personnel, to head hunters and corporate executives and also includes top names from banking, telecommunications, advertising, retailing, politics, sports and entertainment. Names include everyone relevant in the tech space (Zuckerberg, Marc Andreesen, Jack Dorsey, Biz Stone, Larry Page and Sergey Brin—to name a few), to all walks of life—Ed Lee (S.F.'s tech friendly Mayor), Jed York (owner of the 49'ers), Brian Wilson (pitcher of the S.F. Giants) and even Ashton Kutcher and will.i.am (whom he allowed to invest into his fund).

Conway has a multitude of nicknames in the crowd of high profile celebrities and hoodie-sporting tech entrepreneurs, that he is often spotted with. He has been labeled "Head of the Rontourage" (which was given to him by Biz Stone, cofounder of Twitter, after bringing in celebrities like Kanye West or will.i.am to Twitter's offices to treat employees). At first glimpse, Ron does not seem to be the type to fit in with his usual circles. He's in his sixties, a bit overweight with a full head of snow-white hair and dresses like a southern frat boy. Yet

Conway connects worlds, unites ideas, steers capital and places talent. In Malcolm Gladwell's The Tipping Point, Gladwell informs us that "connectors" are people with a special gift for bringing the world together. Conway epitomizes the very definition and is the reason why Marc Andreesen (cofounder of Netscape and partner of prestigious VC firm Andreesen & Horowitz) calls him the "human router." His style is old school and reminiscent of old world mafia. It is the very reason he has earned himself the most grabbing moniker of all as "Silicon Valley's Godfather."

Since the mid 90's Conway has invested in more than 600 internet companies. Hundreds went bust but some have had great success in the dot-com boom. He placed capital in PayPal and Google. In the current social media frenzy he has invested in Groupon, Dropbox, Square, Airbnb and Twitter—which are just the companies who have valuations over $1 billion. He has already sold companies like Zappos and Mint, for a nine-figure investment fund, which emulates the SV Model. Marc Andreesen, an investor of Conway's fund, says the SV Angel Portfolio is among the top performing seed funds in the valley. "If someone were to outperform him in seed investing, it is because they got in on the next Facebook and he hadn't," Andreesen notes. "The people who say 'spray and pray' don't understand the business model," states Lee (Manager of the SV Angel Fund). "They have no idea what they're talking about."

In 2011, SV Angel did something even more audacious to cause envy in the Valley and shake up the seed investment space: it partnered with Yuri Milner and Andreesen. To invest in every startup accepted into the Y Combinator Program. "Y Combinator is the Harvard of accelerators," acknowledges Conway.

Despite all of the criticism Conway receives, he has obviously left a lasting footprint on the entrepreneurs he works with, other investors in the sector—whether friend or foe, and the tech space itself. His core desire to help the entrepreneurs he partners with and go about it by any means possible is unrivaled. "Entrepreneurs, because they need money, they are willing to share their crystal ball with someone like me," he says. "That's the best thing ever."

"Head of the Rontourage," "The Human Router" or the "Silicon Valley Godfather"— whatever you call him has made a name for himself by being the most connected person in the Valley, and appointing himself as the ultimate connector in a vast network of top execs, celebrities, politicians and ambitious tech entrepreneurs. And who could envision a better guardian angel to tech entrepreneurs then Super-angel Ron Conway?

Fortune, The Silicon Valley Startup's Best Friend, February 2012. Miguel Helft

FB: THE HACKER WAY

In March 2012, one in every eight people on the planet used Facebook. The site has transformed giant portions of the economy, has globalized the world like never before, and has even altered the way we conduct our daily lives. In the same month and year, Fortune, thanks to Miguel Helft and Jessi Hempel, gave us an inside look into the social media behemoth that we've never seen before. The story gave us a rare glimpse as to how the company has designed its culture while reinventing the rules of the web, growing at light speed. The article came after Facebook decided to file for its IPO.

At Facebook, there are many ways to solve one problem and everyone is pushed to come up with their own solutions. "The Hacker Way" is not unique to web technology companies—think Google, Zynga, and Intuit, who all practice continuous improvement and fast iteration—yet Zuck's relentless allegiance is what makes the Facebook culture unrivaled. At Facebook, the Hacker Way is everything—it's how the company is organized, how its ranks are managed, and even how employees are trained.

In order for Facebook to maintain its hacker street cred, while experiencing lightning growth, Zuckerberg has had to instruct a unit of highly specialized operators to fill in the role of middle-management, while aspiring to remain flat. He has kept the organization agile and every year or so, engineers are required to leave their teams to work on something different for at least a month. This process brings a fresh perspective to engineering teams and it averts managers from becoming stagnant.

Development teams are kept as small as possible for the greater good of execution and speed. It is the result of the famous "like" button. One of the most important features of Facebook: it was birthed out of a team of just three, a product manager, a designer and a part-time engineer.

In order to familiarize new employees to the Facebook ethos, Facebook takes them through a six-week boot camp. Here, they learn about Facebook's culture by FB veterans and are also given laptops and their desk. Once they login to their laptop for the first time they find six e-mails: one welcomes them to the team, and the other five describe tasks they'll need to perform. "It's terrifying to ship code to FB and to think there are a billion people out there using the service," said Jocelyn Goldfein, an engineering director.

This sink or swim approach empowers new hires to understand the mantra: "Done is better than perfect," and "Move fast and break things."

Nobody personifies the Hacker Way better than Zuck himself. "He's less a dictator than a guru for these coders, and of course his opinion is final. The reason Mark has final word is because he is f*cking brilliant," exclaims Andrew Bosworth, a director of engineering and longtime FB veteran.

In an exclusive 2005 interview, Zuck claimed to be the one who determined to build the site as a "social utility." The way he pushed that idea forward was to turn his website into a platform for third-party applications. In jobs like fashion he not only weighs in on tiny details but will spend time in the trenches implementing them. As Helft and Hempel tell us, "Engineers are romanced by the size and scope of his vision; for many, winning his approval is its own reward."

Zuckerberg delayed an IPO for as long as possible due to a number of primary reasons: one because he was concerned about losing control of his creation, and the second reason is that he didn't want the hacker culture weakened in any way, when opening the FB doors to the public. Zuck successfully hurdled the first obstacle by retaining 22% of the company's equity and 57% of its voting shares. Private or not, it is difficult for any company that matures and grows to stay agile: it happened to Microsoft in the 90's, IBM and Intel. Even Google has resurrected its organization to make executives more accountable, and cut any extra bureaucratic fat.

Despite the obvious crossroads Facebook faces, The Hacker Way—where mock-ups are favored over conversations and code wins arguments—has been the existential contributing factor to its domination. This is an obstacle even Zuck may find hard hacking.

Fortune, Inside Facebook, March 2012. Miguel Helft & Jack Hempel

ENTREPRENEURISM:
WHAT MOTIVATES YOU?

In March 2012, Inc. Magazine wrote an article that highlighted the reasons people start businesses. According to Noah Wassermann, an associate professor at Harvard Business School and guest columnist for Inc., who surveyed 2,000 founders about their motivations to start a company, explains, "One of the key things about entrepreneurs is that they have far more potential to make decisions with both head and heart. When you're taking the world on your shoulders, you have to ask yourself, 'Why am I doing this?' If you only listen to your head, the decisions you make at every fork in the road can drive you farther from your personal promised land."

Wassermann found that autonomy is the number one motivating factor for entrepreneurship of all ages from 20 to 40+ in both men and women. Power and influence also reigned supreme across both genders and ages, except for women 40+ who rated intellectual challenge above power and influence. Other motivating factors were financial gain, managing people, variety and altruism. Altruism only becoming motivating for men ages 40+, while women considered altruism the reason for self-employment at all ages.

The survey was taken as part of a larger self-assessment tool called Career Leader, which is used by hundreds of universities and business schools around the world. Knowing what drives you and makes you tick is critical when making tough decisions. Founders who understand their motivating factors, for starting their companies, are more able to satisfy their individual needs and execute their vision, which contributes to the greater good of all.

Inc. Magazine, March 2012, The Motivation Matrix. Leigh Buchanan

FACEBOOK'S IPO:
PROVING THE IPO MODEL'S BROKEN

2012 will forever be etched into the tech history books as the year the social media juggernaut filed for an IPO whether right or wrong, in victory or defeat—only time will tell. For the record, though Zuck delayed an IPO for as long as possible, as to not lose control of his baby by opening it up to the public, and not dilute the hacker culture he's established and worked so hard to maintain. In April 2012, Felix Salmon of Wired Magazine wrote an article explaining why Wall Street is the tech industry's worst enemy.

As the article states, with Facebook raising $5 billion, it marks the biggest internet IPO the world has ever seen. At its open on the Exchange, FB will be valued more than General Motors, The NY Times Company and Sprint and Nextel combined. The IPO was not by choice though, but because stipulations in the SEC rules state that once a company takes on more than 500 shareholders—which Facebook definitely surpasses once you add up founders, investors (early and late) and employees who have purchased or received shares throughout the years—it must register its stock. As soon as a company registers its stock, shareholders then have the right to trade stock on the OTC (over the counter) markets, which are secondary markets, that typically garner lower valuations for the company and shares are traded out of the company's control.

Fortunately, for future tech CEO's, the SEC may not have the power to corner companies into an IPO by their sheer number of shareholders. At the time of the Wired article writing, bills have been presented to Congress, which demand legislation to raise the shareholder limit to 1,000 versus the current 500 mark. The bills have been supported quite vocally by pre-IPO CEOs, professional tech investors and Silicon Valley as a whole.

Unfortunately, this is not the case for Zuck and Facebook. Clearly, he understands the obstacles an IPO presents to Facebook itself—by forcing him to focus on short-term stock volatility by sacrificing long-term growth to appease the market, and relinquishing control from founders while passing it to shareholders. Due to his foresight, he has been able to establish safeguards—like controlling 50 percent of the voting shares, the ability to appoint directors without anyone's consent and will even be able to name his successor—that should empower FB a smooth IPO. But, as Felix Salmon wrote in the article, "When the world's most successful young tech entrepreneur does everything in his power to minimize the impact of public ownership, it makes one thing clear: the IPO model is broken."

Historically in America, from the 1930's to the late 90's, the initial public offering drove our nation's capitalistic economy. Investors purchased shares from entrepreneurs, who in turn used the capital to build their companies. Microsoft and Apple are prime examples, who, post-IPO, had enough cash to develop Windows and the Macintosh. That was a valuable service IPOs provided, but it's no longer the case. Strict Sarbanes-Oxley laws have made going public harder, and today's investors prefer to see proven track records of steady profitability thus creating a Catch-22. Well, if IPO's do not provide hot startups the necessary funds to build their companies, that begets the question—what purpose do IPOs provide today's tech darlings?

Primarily, in today's tech ecosystem, the IPO has provided founders and early investors a means to cashing out. Wait, a means to cashing out? Let's step back and analyze what that means for a moment—first, after a company goes public, the demand for constant growth is heightened. There is more pressure from external forces (new shareholders) and the founding team typically loses some control of important decision-making authority. In other words, founders who typically have a clear, long-term vision of their company, whose primary motivations for being self-employed are autonomy, power and influence, end up having to put their long-term visions in the backseat to the marketplace's short-term demands to hit their numbers every quarter, end up working for their shareholders, and having already cashed-out—are no longer motivated by the allure of vast riches through company stock ownership. To state it simply, post-IPO teams have very little incentive to continue pouring blood, sweat and tears into a company that is barely theirs any longer.

It's not until you look under the hood that you see how broken the current IPO vehicle truly is. Granted, cashing out founders and investors is good for founders and investors, but it does not provide value to the company itself. So what are the options?

Assuming the bills get passed through legislation, at least the SEC will not have the power to force companies into going public. And, new approaches to funding make it easier for private companies to sell equity and raise capital—namely, crowdfunding. Hello Kickstarter. In addition, the most viable alternative to an IPO is for companies to enter the private markets. The private markets are online portals (like SecondMarket and SharesPost) that allow companies to trade their stock without public scrutiny (which is different than the OTC markets). There are a multitude of benefits the private markets offer, and private companies have reaped the value. Since 2008, more than $1 billion of stock have changed hands on SecondMarket, which is the largest of the private markets. The private markets offer a real solution to the IPO, and I would imagine the industry will continue to see an increase in the use of these markets.

If in fact, the IPO model cannot be fixed, and tech companies will have to continue testing innovative strategies to fundraising and new technologies. Fortunately, for the sector as a whole, tech entrepreneurs have shown a bit of resiliency over the years. And, in seeing as how a broken IPO model brings opportunity for entrepreneurs to create business to address the obstacle, wouldn't it be ironic if the answer to the problem came in the form of the next hottest tech startup?

Wired Magazine, April 2012, Why Going Public Sucks. Felix Salmon

BEN SILBERMANN:
THE PINTEREST EFFECT

In March 2012, Pinterest arose as the fastest-growing website of all time. The site registered 17.8 million users that month, according to ComScore, which equated to a 52 percent increase in just one month—and wasn't even open to everyone (would be "pinners" still had to request to join). In February, Pinterest drove more traffic to websites than Twitter, Google+, LinkedIn and YouTube combined, and the success resulted in Fortune publishing an article in April 2012.

Pinterest is an uncontrollably addicting social media platform that has users ("pinners") sharing images on web-based pinboards. Big and small brands alike have scrambled to establish their presence on the site, in order for users to "pin" their products, which acts as a referral for the user's followers who then can click on their product "pins," to learn more about those products.

Pinterest's surge in growth isn't just due to their unique celebrity endorsers—like Mitt Romney's wife, Ann, organizing family photos on the site, or Reese Witherspoon confessing her love for the site on Late Night with Conan O' Brian. Nor, is it solely based on the $27 million capital infusion from one of the most influential VC firms in the Valley—Andreesen Horowitz—that Pinterest received in October, 2011, valuing the upstart for a reported $200 million. The growth is not even the result of the United States Army publishing a guide for how to use the site. In fact, these incidents are simply a result of the value Pinterest provides. What has set Pinterest apart and has primarily contributed to its explosive growth is that historically, a technology's early adopters are male tech enthusiasts from either side of the coast, but Pinterest has found its most loyal disciples among scrapbooking females from the Mid-West. Plus, Pinterest has another unique quality—it is very good at helping discover new things, with personalized recommendations. Search sites are good tools for helping you find something you can name, while social media sites are helpful in facilitating conversation, but, not necessarily good at providing new recommendations. Pinterest has been able to fill that void by cross-pollinating social media with search.

The hyper-growth has catapulted Ben Silbermann, 29 at the time, CEO and cofounder, into the limelight. He fell in love with the tech space after stumbling across TechCrunch. This occurred around 2003 while working for a consulting company in D.C. after graduating college. He knew something major was going on in Silicon Valley and wanted to be a part of it. He says, "It felt like this was the story of my time and I just wanted to be close to it."

So he packed up and headed west to Palo Alto, where he landed a sales job at Google. Not surprisingly—he credits Google with pushing him to dream huge and push his own limits. And he did—in 2008; he took the entrepreneurial dive, lassoed some college buddies and started spitballing startup concepts. Silbermann has always been obsessed with collecting things and the team ran with the idea to turn the hobby into a social site. Silbermann's wife came up with the name, and by January 2010, the team began e-mailing friends and family to invite them to try the service. At first, it was growing slow and four months in, the site had just a few hundred users. But, then, something happened; a tipping point that changed everything. Once the Pinterest growth engine started moving, it didn't stop. Since inception, the site has added an estimated 40 to 50 percent more users each month. The speed of adoption has trumped all major tech players in history. The site's approximate time generating 50,000 to 17 million monthly unique visitors has been staggering in an astounding 9 months (May 2011 to February 2012) compared to Tumblr which took 30 months to reach that milestone, Twitter at 22, Facebook 16 and YouTube at 12.

In spite of all the current success and pressure of running the Valley's "it" startup, Silbermann has been able to keep his cool. His team lives by the FB ethos of "Move Fast and Break Things." He speaks of Pinterest the way someone talks about a priceless piece of art, "When you open Pinterest, it should feel like someone has hand-made a book for you. Every item should feel like it's handpicked for you by a person you care about."

Silbermann understands that the immediate growth alone does not ensure long-term success. He realizes how he must build a company that can manage the hypergrowth, and determine the monetization strategy. He understands that the more traction Pinterest garners, the more time his site would take away from other, larger more notable social media sites (eh hem Facebook) making him a serious target. He knows with such low barriers to entry, new social sites pop up all the time, creating new threats. And, he knows no matter how many times Reese Witherspoon goes on Conan that these are the obstacles he faces as the result of creating something people actually want. And, as told to Jessi Hempel of Fortune magazine, Silbermann says the feeling is "the intersection on the Venn diagram of fear and joy."

Fortune Magazine, April 2012, Is Pinterest the Next Facebook? Jessi Hempel

CONNECTOMICS: MAKING DUMB NEURONS SMART AND THE WORLD A MORE INTELLIGENT PLACE

Sebastian Seung, a professor of computational neuroscience in MIT's Department of Brain and Cognitive Sciences, wants to figure out how to enable computers to connect our thoughts. His fusion of theoretical physics and human intelligence has given him a unique perspective in exploring a growing field called Connectomics—which is the mapping and study of neural networks. The new discipline could one day lead to a better grasp of how memory personalities and pathologies all work.

The current process of mapping neural networks is a painstakingly slow process and took scientists more than a decade to map the connections between 300 neurons in a tiny worm. The human brain has a hundred billion neurons. With the goal to expedite the process and contribute to his work, Seung has developed computer-vision algorithms that vocalize the boundaries between individual neurons, making it easier to map the networks.

His work has contributed immensely to the growing field, and he has written a book called "Connectome," which shares his studies. He feels, "We should ask not what the brain can do for the computer, but ask what the computer can do for the brain."

He hopes to someday answer the question—"How do you take dumb neurons and put them together to make an intelligent mind?" If he does in fact, successfully solve the riddle, one thing is certain, he won't have a shortage of customers that could benefit through his work. Plus, it sounds like a recession-proof business model. Cheers to his success in figuring out how to make the world a more intelligent place—God knows, we could use it.

Wired, April 2012, Map Quest. Matthew Hutson

REID HOFFMAN: OXFORD PHILOSOPHER TURNED TECH INTELLIGENT

Reid Hoffmann, LinkedIn founder, Digg, Zynga, Friendster, Flickr, Airbnb investor, Groupon adviser (and investor), was actually asked to lead Facebook's first funding round by Sean Parker. After passing it onto his Stanford College pal Peter Thiel, he calls the decision to pass "the most expensive decision of his life." The scenario itself displays his power and influence in the tech sphere (and, all things did not end horribly for Reid, he did actually make a 5 figure investment, although his ownership percentage is unknown).

All his early life, Hoffman dreamed of becoming a philosopher. After Stanford, he went to Oxford to study great ideas and figure out how to strengthen public intellectual culture. However, within months at Oxford he determined spending his life answering one question would not leave enough impact. He realized it was the wrong platform—not enough scalability. So, he became a software entrepreneur instead.

He started his first business in 1997—a dating site called Socialnet.Com, that attracted $1.7 million in venture capital funding but never really got off the ground—before joining a company Peter Thiel founded called "Confinity" in 2000, the company which was originally focused on mobile encryption, pivoted to online payments and merged with Elon Musk's X.Com to become the legendary PayPal.Com.

In 2003, he cofounded LinkedIn, and served as CEO until 2007, before relinquishing power to serve as Executive Chair. Peter Thiel (PayPal cofounder, lead FB funder and preeminent Valley moneyman) and Hoffman, have been close friends since their undergrad days at Stanford. Thiel has been quoted to have remembering a conversation they had in college about the meaning of life and says, "Reid's answer was that it's the people you spend your life with—the connections you make. It's no surprise that Reid thought through social networking more methodically than anyone else did." LinkedIn stands largely unchallenged as the go-to business social-media platform. In April 2012, the site boasted of more than 150 million accounts—growing at about two new members per second. Yet, Reid claims few truly understand its value—not just a place to schmooze and network, but a place to get business intelligence, to research problems, and truly establish an online footprint where other people in the network can find them. He claims that, "If Americans really learned how to use LinkedIn, it would raise the country's GDP."

In May, 2011, LinkedIn went public at a $4.3 billion valuation; within hours, the stock price rocketed from $45 to $94.25 and helped catapult him to the Forbes' list, estimating his net worth to be $1.5 billion. And although he is known for his modest reputation—he drove the same green Acura for 10 years that he bought when PayPal was sold, while Thiel purchased a Ferrari—his wealth substantiates his value in the tech world.

Joi Ito (co-investor of over 20 deals) says, "Reid looks at the world and society as a huge game, an intellectual exercise where he's trying to optimize for the common good." The would-be philosopher has big visions—Big Data as "Web 3.0," the true power of more computing and "biology as code"—and may have in a roundabout way, set out to accomplish exactly what he imagined he would as a philosopher. "The future," he says, "is sooner and stranger than you think."

Wired Magazine, April, 2012, The Social Networker. David Rowan

WIRED MAGAZINE: THE 7 LAWS OF DIVINATION

In May 2012, Wired published an article titled "How to Spot the Future," which provided Wired's 7 rules for identifying the trends, technologies and ideas that will change the world. I perceive value in their 7 rules and can see examples of their laws being used in the industry. Being a tech entrepreneur myself, I'm constantly seeking ways to stay ahead of the curve and found the article very insightful. Their 7 rules are: look for cross-pollinators, surf the exponentials, favor the liberators, give points for audacity, bank on openness, demand deep design and spend time with time wasters. Wired has been covering the tech sector for 20 years and with articles like this one, have legitimately established their authority in the space. Wired claims, "that these 7 rules have allowed them to size up ideas and separate the truly world-changing from the merely interesting. That any story they publish, any idea deemed transformative, any trend that has legs, draws one or more of these core principles. That they have played a major part in creating the world we see today. And they'll be the forces behind the world we'll be living tomorrow." You can judge the validity of their rules yourself.

1. <u>Look for Cross-pollinators</u>: Granted, an idea can transfer from one industry to another, but true cross-pollination occurs at inception, not just application. For instance, when mathematician John Von Neumann infused human strategy and mathematics, game theory was born. When he combined engineering and physics, he created computer science. Wired says that cross-pollination can be potent enough to generate entirely new disciplines. Case in point, behavioral economics was developed when two psychiatrists attempted to answer why people didn't behave rationally. Or, how about this—crossing code between digital technology and biology has given us a whole new breed of fields: Computational Genomics, Systems Biology, Synthetic Biology and Bioinformatics. The bottom-line is that intertwining different disciplines can equate to a stronger sum than each part on its own. One plus one, can in fact equal three.

2. <u>Surf the Exponentials</u>: Exponentials in this context are better defined as "disruptive technologies." Obviously, this is not a new concept—Clayton Christensen's "The

Innovator's Dilemma" substantiates the value in disruptive technologies, and claims it is these technologies that open established markets, thus creating the new norm in that space, until a new disruptor knocks off the previous, resulting in a continuous cycle. Moore's Law—that "chips" will exponentially get smaller, faster, and cheaper—is a prime example of disruptive technology in action. Take the first iPod from 2001, for instance, which had 5 gigabytes for $399, and then fast forward 10 plus years to today's "classic" model that boasts of 160 gigs at $249—which equates to a 51-fold upgrade. YouTube was birthed when the team realized broadband was becoming so inexpensive and commonplace that it was on the cusp of changing the way people viewed online videos. The team surfed that disruptive wave to the bank and cashed out through a Google acquisition. Dropbox rode the cloud storage surge while watching the cost of disc space drop exponentially. In other words, have a keen sense of the sector's present capabilities and watch for visionaries who are advancing the space with new technologies.

3. <u>Favor the Liberators</u>: As Wired describes, liberators can be those who either 1: use technology to access goods which were previously not available (think MP3s which untethered music from CD) or 2: use technology to put sleeping assets to work (see Uber who has turned idling cab drivers into on-demand cabs, or Airbnb who has transformed unused homes into temporary lodging). Liberators see opportunity in obstacles, and liberate us from complacency.

4. <u>Give points for Audacity</u>: Audacious entrepreneurial visions change the world we know. Look at Zuck's mission to make the world more connected; look at what Jobs did to the music, PC and movie (Pixar) industries. One of my favorite audacious stories is about Elon Musk deciding to colonize Mars. He went on NASA's website to see the date in which it was to take place, found nothing, and realized there were no plans to do so. Rather than sit around and wonder why—he created SpaceX to carry out the task himself. Why not dream out of this world? Worst case you fail—and failure is expected in order to produce disruptive innovation.

5. <u>Bank on Openness</u>: Yes, we are talking transparency, collaboration and bottom-up innovation. Openness can transform industries—a strong example is open source coding. Previously, open source software was a low-grade way of developing, but has since become the golden standard of the industry with even major players like IBM, Google and Microsoft on board. Another example is the inception of crowdfunding and crowdsourcing being the product of openness, these disciplines have unlocked unrivaled power in collaboration.

6. <u>Demand Deep Design</u>: Steve Jobs was a relentless advocate for deep design in the form of simplicity. He claimed, "Simplicity is the ultimate sophistication," which seemed to be a decent strategy seeing as how Apple is the most valuable company on the planet. With the advent of design thinking as a primary function of business, rather than a secondary, it seems the business world understands that design must be an intrinsic attribute in order to achieve success.

7. <u>Spend Time with Time Wasters</u>: Here's an awesome example—people addicted to playing Angry Birds. I'm confident you knew at least one junkie with the same problem. This may seem trivial on the surface, but if you look at what Zynga was able to accomplish with the game, you'll see the underlying value. You see, through Angry Birds (the mobile app version) Zynga evolved the entire gaming industry to mobile versus console. Zynga was able to do this by simply capturing the attention of time wasters. Social media is another great example of creating an industry so powerful we can learn what someone is doing every minute of the day (thank you oversharers).

These rules alone, obviously, do not invent the future, but when visionaries can harness the power they unleash, amazing occurrences happen. Industries can be upended, technology can advance faster than we can envision and our daily lives will be enhanced exponentially.

Clearly, these 7 rules have made Wired Magazine the most formidable publication in the tech sector, with an unparalleled insight into not only the underpinnings of present tech trends but the predictive power of future disruption.

Wired Magazine, May, 2012, How to Spot the Future. Thomas Goetz

DAVE MCCLURE: SITH LORD ROCKSTAR OF 500 STARTUPS

Dave McClure is scrubbing the world for up and coming startups. In the past 3 years, he has visited 30 cities, including New Delhi, Shanghai, Amsterdam, Prague and Honolulu.

Dave is no stranger to the startup world, and claims his own experience made him empathetic to startups. In 1988, after graduating from college, he found work as a software developer then started his own e-commerce site. He later landed a gig at PayPal where he was a project manager. After PayPal's 2002 IPO, he took $300,000 of his profits to place small investments in 13 tech startups, most notably Mint.Com (acquired by Intuit in 2009) and SlideShare, which LinkedIn purchased. From there, while working at the San Francisco based venture capital firm, Founders Fund, was then asked to run the Facebook fbFund, which invests in companies developing apps for the social media giant, and transitioned yet again.

The culmination of his success, and the desire to fill an important need in the industry empowered him to create his fund—500 Startups, while earning him the unique title as "Sith Lord of the Fund." 500 Startups provides seed stage investments from $10,000 to $25,000, along with mentorship from tech execs, attorneys and venture capitalists, work space at the 500 Startups' 100,000-square-foot Silicon Valley dig and peer-to-peer networking from other companies in residence. "Instead of just giving them money, they give them space, mentors and coaching. It's like a minor league that feeds players into the bigger VC system," states Jeff Cornwall, a professor of entrepreneurship at Belmont University in Nashville.

Author of critically acclaimed tech textbook, "The Four Steps to the Epiphany," visionary, and investor of 500 Startups, Steve Blank says, "Dave gets it. He has a knack for finding and nurturing companies that are too small to command attention from traditional VCs."

The fund has invested in 300 companies, which includes Farmeron, a Croatian company that develops software to help farmers organize data on their livestock, and Mexico's Ovia, which empowers companies to set up video interviews of job candidates. Also, on the list are Punchd and TeachStreet, which were acquired by Google and Amazon. "Seeding numerous small investments around the world makes sense," Dave says, "because at least 75 percent of tech startups don't survive longer than three years. Some folks call this 'spray and pray,' but we call it going global, and not wasting money at failing. Fail on a small budget and you save a lot of money and heartbreak. We're one of the few VC firms to get outside a 30-mile radius of sand hill road."

And, so began the three-year-old dog and pony show McClure calls geeks on a plane. "McClure is becoming an entrepreneurship rock star in countries like Brazil and India," says Vivek Wadhwa, a former software developer.

Traveling outside the 30-mile sand hill road radius is an understatement—in addition to the past 30 cities he and his team visited over the past 3 years, the geeks plan to descend on Tallinn, Berlin, Moscow, Dubai, Istanbul, Tel Aviv, Amman and cities in sub-Saharan Africa. With so much diversity, so many unique perspectives, and so much startup activity, it's hard to imagine Dave's vision will not be successful. At the very least, he will have enlarged his territory, established world-wide connections and will have seen parts of the world even a rock star would envy.

Bloomberg BusinessWeek, May-June 2012, An American Idol for Entrepreneurship. Roben Farzad

TECHSHOP:
CATALYST TO THE DIY REVOLUTION

Need to build a robot? How about an iPad case? What about a device to run credit cards via cellphone, to disrupt the outdated cash register industry—enter Square? Maybe a laser hair loss treatment helmet, a folding kayak, jet pack, infant warmer, electronic motorcycle, or even a Super Mario Brothers question mark lamp, that marks the same noise when you hit a cube in the video game? (Note: all are products that have been created at Techshop). Well then, do what the geeks in Silicon Valley do and head over to your neighborhood Techshop.

Techshop is the Promised Land for anyone who likes to build things. The average Techshop facility is about 17,000 square feet and has all types of equipment and machinery—sewing machines, mills, metal lathes, and high-priced computer machines that cut precise patterns out of slabs of metal. $100 a month gets you membership into the exclusive club and access to all the equipment. A few bucks more and you can attend a variety of classes from computer drafting 3D models to beginner's welding.

There are three Techshops in the Bay Area, one in Raleigh, N.C., another in Detroit thanks to a partnership with Ford, and (in May/June 2012) plans to open shops in Austin, Phoenix, New York, Los Angeles, Boston, Chicago, Seattle and San Diego. Each Techshop has a different look and feel. As the May-June 2012, Bloomberg BusinessWeek issue tells us, the Menlo Park Techshop opened in 2006, as part of a boomlet in so-called hacker spaces. Lacking garage workshops, city dwellers created places where they can write software code or build robots, while socializing and sharing their expertise. They make up what's called "The Maker Movement"—do-it-yourself zealots who claim they meet a fundamental human need by building things with their hands. And, Techshop acts as a main facilitator in the movement—the treehouse of the secret club.

In 2006, Jim Newton, vet of the Silicon Valley's hardware scene and previous advisor to the Mythbuster's television series, announced his plans to launch the first shop in Menlo Park after teaching a machine class. The response was staggering as interested DIY'ers handed him membership dues on the spot, while more people offered cash to be investors, and Newton effortlessly raised the needed $350,000 to open the first shop. More sites were started in a similar fashion as Mark Hatch, CEO of Techshop, has tried to fund each location through local investors. However, he quickly realized it was a slow process and it stalled growth. The team has since established that through corporate sponsors, each location can reach profitability quicker. Membership has grown to about 3,300 and Techshop projections are planned to break even at each site this year (2012). Through its corporate sponsorship program, each sponsor guarantees a certain number of members. Mark Hatch has additional dreams to add-on to the Techshop locations. He'd like to add service desks where members can send a file, and Techshop will 3D print the object or laser cut it, and members will simply pick it up—offering an almost Kinko's-like service for the Maker Movement.

The Techshop shot has not just been heard in the Valley, and a very important partner from Washington D.C. has stepped forward. The Defense Department disclosed that it will place $3.5 million to fund two Techshops—one near Washington D.C. and the other in Pittsburg. Regular members will work in the day while employees of the Defense Advanced Research Projects Agency (DARPA) will arrive at midnight to execute after-hours work. Their mission is to design factories that can be reconfigured on the fly and dubbed "Project i-Fab." "Darpa has invested in Techshop as part of a larger vision: to see if citizens can out-invent military contractors on some of its more out-of-the-box assignments.

As Bloomberg BusinessWeek says, "For some, Techshop represents a raised fist in the age of Made in China—and an opportunity to opt out of mass-market consumption and unleash their own creativity. Techshop has quickly become an epicenter for DIY enthusiasts where members can iterate rapidly, turn ideas to products immediately and harness the collective experiences, expertise and ambition of the movement. Techshop represents more than just a paradise for DIY'ers, but embodies the maker revolution as a whole while it acts as the central command station for the troops.

Bloomberg BusinessWeek, May 28-June 3, 2012, The Makers. Ashlee Vance

MARC ANDREESSEN: THE ALL-KNOWING

In May 2012, while preparing for its 20th anniversary in January 2013, Wired Magazine launched a series called "Wired Icons." The series included in-depth interviews with their biggest heroes—who built digital culture and evangelized it over the past two decades.

And, no one is a better selection than Marc Andreesen—whose singular visions have transformed the way we communicate through technology more than a handful of times. At 22 years old, he created Mosaic, the first browser, an invention that single-handedly introduces the Internet to hundreds of millions of households. He cofounded Netscape and took it public via one of the largest internet IPO's at that time. Years ahead of the curve, he created LoudCloud, an innovative company that brought cloud computing to business. And as of recent, has created the most paramount venture capital fund in the world, which has backed notable promising Web 2.0 companies—from Twitter, to Groupon, Skype, Airbnb and Instagram.

For the Wired Icon interview, Editor-In-Chief Chris Anderson spoke with Andreesen's office in Palo Alto, about the five powerful ideas Andreesen had before anyone else. The following are excerpts from that interview.

In 1992, as a 22-year-old undergrad, at the University of Illinois, Marc had his first big vision—he knew everyone would have access to the web, it was just a matter of when, which contributed to him developing Mosaic, the first graphical browser for the Internet. His vision was birthed from two unique experiences: one was the fact that he came from a very small town in Wisconsin with three TV networks, two radio stations and no cable TV. He came from a place where he was starved for information and hungry for connection. The second was, while at college in Illinois, he had access to a supercomputer, where he found the Internet that made information so abundant. At the university, he was on the Internet in a way that was very modern, even by today's standards, and was convinced everyone would want to be connected and have that experience for themselves.

Through these unique experiences, the Mosaic browser was birthed. Mosaic created a snowball effect of incidents that led to a wide adoption of consumer internet use. First was the simple fact that Mosaic made the Internet much easier to use, and making it easier to use led to the realization of how to use it—all the things people could do with it—which made people want it more. Andreesen comments, "It's also clear that we helped drive faster bandwidth: by creating the demand, we helped increase the supply."

Through the awakening that everyone would be connected through the web, Andreesen viewed the Internet in macro-economic terms—international trade and globalization. He understood that, "If everybody gets Internet, they end up with a browser so they not only look at web pages—but they also leave comments, and create web pages. They can even host their own server! So not only is everybody consuming, they can also provide. And once you get instantaneous communication with everybody, you have economic activity far more advanced, far more liquid, and far more distributed than ever before."

In 1995, following the massive success of Mosaic, Andreesen had his second glimpse of the future when he predicted that the browser would be the operating system. Granted, this vision has taken almost 15 years to come to fruition, versus the year his first idea , took. And, with new hardware to solve the problem—in smartphones and tablets, where the operating system (Google Chrome OS and Apple's iOS, for instance) is a fully functional browser-based operating system that houses applications (e-mail to social media, etc.) entirely on the network. Andreesen reflects that the idea they had then, which seems obvious today, was to lift the computing off of each user's device and perform it in the network instead. It's something he thinks is inherent in the technology—what some thinkers refer to as the "technological imperative." It's as if the technology wants it to happen. He says that technology is like water; it wants to find its level. If you hook up your computer to a billion other computers, it just makes sense that a tremendous share of the resources you want to use—not only text or media but processing power too—will be located remotely. Andreesen states that it makes sense if you look at the web like this: "That the web is about accessing applications. Think of each website as an application, and every single click, every single interaction with that site, is an opportunity to be on the latest version of that application. Once you start thinking in terms of networks, it just doesn't make sense to prefer local apps, with downloadable installing code that needs to be constantly updated."

And, that's exactly what he set out to accomplish with Netscape—to enable the browser to do more. It was also the goal of JavaScript, which he invented to pair with the Netscape browser that empowered far more sophisticated applications in the network by building support into the browser. The basic premise, which is still prevalent today, is that you do some computing on the device, but you want the server application to be in total control of the process and the whole process is invisible to the user. A prime example of this type of computing is smartphones and tablets which are the network computers Andreesen envisioned all those years ago.

As for the future of the web, Andreesen foresees the web application model. The apps will live on the web, because the technology wants it to work that way.

In 1999, idea three was to capitalize on the thought that his company LoudCloud would empower businesses to relocate to the cloud; LoudCloud would host and manage their web services and software so their clients would not need to run any servers at all. Despite early success and an IPO in 2001, LoudCloud rebranded, changed its business model in 2002, and sold to Hewlett-Packard in 2007. Andreesen claims that Loudcloud was five or six years too early for two primary reasons. The first was commodization: they were running on expensive Sun servers, but people now can buy Linux servers at a fraction of the cost. The second was virtualization: which makes managing the servers and apportioning services to clients far easier than was possible back in 1999. To better understand LoudCloud and its mission, Andreesen likes to refer to an electrical metaphor: "When electricity first came to factories, every factory had its own generator. But eventually, that didn't make sense, because everyone could draw electricity off the grid. At the height of the first dotcom boom, we saw the exact same thing happening in Silicon Valley. You'd raise $20 million of venture capital, and then you'd have to turn around and write $5 million checks to Oracle, Sun, EMC and Cisco just to build your server farm. It was literally like everybody building their own electrical generator over and over again. By capitalizing on economies of scale, LoudCloud could provide higher levels of service than you could get in-house, and a startup could get its product to market almost immediately."

And that's why Amazon's cloud service and all other cloud service providers today have been so effective. Andreesen says, "It's all the same core concept—but with super-cheap hardware which makes the economies far more attractive for everybody and with virtualization, which makes the entire environment far more adaptable.

In 2004, while Facebook was just a gleam in a Harvard sophomore's eye as Andreesen puts it, he knew everything would be social. In the 90's while everyone was obsessed with Moore's Law—which predicts that processing speed will increase exponentially, and Metcalfe's Law—which dictates that network gets more valuable as nodes are applied, Andreesen was intrigued by Reed's Law. "Reed's Law is a mathematical property about the forming of groups—for any group of size N, the number of subgroups that can be assembled is 2."

Through this premonition, he cofounded Ning, which let groups of people create their own social apps. Ning was a modest success but blazed the path for all of today's prominent social sites—from Facebook to Instagram and even Groupon and the founders of the aforementioned list understand Andreesen's value and foresight because he is an investor or board member of each of their companies.

In 2009, Andreesen and his longtime business partner Ben Horowitz created a throwback Silicon Valley venture capital fund called Andreesen Horowitz. Their plan was to capitalize on the vision of an economy transformed by the rise of computing. As Chris Anderson writes, Andreesen believes that enormous technology companies can be built around the use of hyperintelligent software to revolutionize whole sectors of the economy from retail to real estate to healthcare. Their focus was to invest in companies primarily based in Silicon Valley that were based on computer science, in what they dubbed "primary technology" companies. The whole premise of a primary technology company is that it's a tech company—a company where, if all the coders quit tomorrow, you'd have to shut down the company.

Andreesen's basic insight is that software is eating the world. That the Internet has spread to the size and scope where it has become economically viable to build huge companies in single domains, where their basic, world changing innovation rests entirely in the code. Andreesen notes that technology has been just a slice of the economy; that we've been making the building blocks to get us to today, while technology is poised to make the whole economy. Especially huge swaths of the economy that historically have not been addressable by technology—think the financial service sector, healthcare, and government. But, ultimately, as Andreesen so effortlessly puts it, "The then what's next is whatever we invent next."

Wired Magazine, May 2013, The Man Who Knows What's Next, Chris Anderson

KLOUT: PROVIDING DAVID A SLINGSHOT

Your online influence can now be measured by a single number. Klout.com is a service that attempts to measure users' social media influence on a scale of 1 to 100.

Just as Google's search engine ranks web pages, Klout is on a mission to rank each person's influence online. The algorithms crawl across the web combing through social media data. So, if you have a public Twitter account, you have a Klout score, whether you know it or not (unless you're actively opted out of Klout's site). Klout scores are then calculated by a myriad of variables including number of followers of all social media sites linked to the user's Klout account. Frequency of updates, the Klout scores of your friends and followers, and the number of likes, retweets and shares that your updates receive.

Klout has quickly infiltrated our everyday transactions. More than 5,000 companies from Disney to Audi, to Turner Broadcasting have already tapped market-leader Klout to identify influencers. Matt Thompson, Klout's VP of platform, says that a number of major companies—airlines, big-box retailers, hospitality brands—are discussing how best to use Klout scores. Soon, he predicts, people with formidable Klout will board planes earlier, get free access to VP airport lounges, stay in better hotel rooms and receive deep discounts from retail stores and flash-sale outlets. "We say to brands that these are the people they should pay attention to most. How they want to do it is up to them," Thompson says.

Klout founder and CEO Jose Fernandez, seems to be blazing a new industry that appears to be promising. Fernandez sees social media as an unprecedented eruption of opinions and microinfluence, a place where the most valuable form of marketing—word of mouth—can be spread farther and faster than the world has ever seen. Prior to social media, there was no way to identify society's hidden influences—"citizen influencers." Fernandez says that he sees Klout as a form of empowerment for the little guy. "This is the democratization of influence. Suddenly, regular people can carve out a niche by creating content that moves quickly through an engaged network. For brands, that's buzz and for the first time in history, we can measure it," says Mark Schaefer, a professor at Rutgers.

Clearly, brands see value in Klout and the VCs in the Valley see value in Klout—it is reported that the startup received a rumored $30 million from prominent VCs like Kleiner

Perkins Caulfield & Byers and Venrock. Some, reserve hesitation for a social media ranking site that places "higher influencer status" on a pop tween than the leader of the free world (Justin Bieber scores a perfect 100 versus Obama's 91). But, hey, you can't please everyone.

Wired Magazine, May 2012, Popularity Counts. Seth Stevenson
Wall Street Journal Newspaper, April 2012, The Days of Klout and Clawback. John Bussey

ZUCK THE HACKER: AND, THE 5 HACKS THAT CHANGED IT ALL

You know what's cool? $20.3 billion dollars. Which is what Zuckerberg stood to gain, assuming the FB IPO hit $10 billion, which would catapult Zuck to becoming one of the top 30 richest people in the world. Who else stood to get rich? Peter Thiel (early FB investor) would earn $1.7 billion for a $500,000 investment, DST and Yuri Milner would make $4.99 billion, the prestigious VC firm Andreesen Horowitz would garner $187.6 million, Sean Parker (who inspired Zuck to retain control of the company through an unusual governance structure) $2.65 billion, Reid Hoffman, cofounder of LinkedIn decided to keep his investment small because the two social services could be seen as competitors and earned a modest $179.1 million, even David Choe (a graffiti artist who painted murals at Facebook's early offices) was paid in stock and would receive $208.4 million.

In a very cool article, written by Brad Stone and Douglas Macmillan of Bloomberg BusinessWeek in May 2012, they explain how this kid programmer was able to "hack the valley" and create the social media colossus Facebook has become. They claim that Zuckerberg and his crew made a series of high-risk moves—five "hacks" that changed Silicon Valley forever—and were far bolder than just sporting a hoodie to his IPO roadshow. The article touches on the five different hacks that has set Facebook apart and contributed to its digital dominance.

Hack #1: Friend the enemy of your enemy, even if that means hooking up with Microsoft. In 2007, Facebook was experiencing exponential user growth but had yet to completely figure out its advertising platform, which was needed to fund its growing staff and infrastructure. At the time, FB had a partnership with Microsoft that enabled the software company to sell banner ads in the U.S., but Zuck needed to extend its capabilities to the rest of the world.

Both Google and Microsoft wanted to win FB's business for the advertising deal and desired the right to make an investment in the upstart. Simultaneously, Zuck skillfully pitted Google and Microsoft against each other, which increased the value of the ad deal and equity investment. Zuck correctly assumed that Google would soon see promise in creating their own social networking website (hello Google+), and simply played the two competitors against each other as a negotiation tactic; Understanding that going with Google would eventually create conflict, he chose Microsoft instead. Microsoft CEO Steve Balmer, agreed to place $240 million in Facebook, at the then-out-of-this-world valuation of $15 billion, which was the highest amount he could invest without getting clearance from his Board of Directors.

Hack #2: Find low maintenance overseas investors instead of know-it-all Americans. Facebook's explosive growth required additional resources, resources primarily being cash. Unfortunately, in 2007, at the height of the housing crisis, U.S. investment funds were retrenching. Fortunately, Zuck didn't even plan on taking the traditional sand hill road, valley-based, venture capital ride anyway. Too many strings came attached with that money—seats on the board, decision-making authority and first right of refusal clauses on future liquidity events—Zuck had no interest in shaping decision-making and was not willing to give up any board seats. So Facebook went overseas, and raised capital from Hong Kong industrialist Li Ka-Shing and German internet entrepreneurs the Samwer brothers. Facebook continued on its off-beaten investment road when it turned down investment offers from General Atlantic and Technology Crossover Ventures (two prominent U.S. private equity funds). And, instead, did a deal with Digital Sky Technologies, whose primary backer Alisher Usmanov had alleged connections to the Kremlin and made his fortune during the fall of the Soviet Union. DST invested $400 million for 2 percent equity, which valued FB at $10 billion (the recession depressed FB's precious valuation of $15 billion). DST brought additional problem-solving and value through buying one large block of employee stock. Early investors and FB employees were already beginning to sell their shares on private exchanges like Secondmarket without the company's consent. However, with buyers obtaining equity this way, Facebook was in danger of prematurely crossing the 500 shareholder threshold which if crossed, the SEC would require it to go public. DST's funding was a controlled strategy to bring in fresh capital while quenching the thirst of shareholders to cash out a portion of their holdings. In one fell swoop, Zuck raised necessary funding, pleased shareholders, further delayed a time consuming IPO and introduced a vast new source of cash to the Valley.

Hack #3: Hire a deputy who completes you. Since inception, Zuck has sought to build a youthful company that understands and embraces future technological advancements. His long term vision of the Internet has been that users will be more open to sharing personal information with new social media sites popping up all the time. He refused to put old fashioned voices on his own management team and turned down big name executives who were introduced by early investors, which is the typical path promising growing startups, are encouraged to pursue. Earlier, in 2008, he personally recruited Sheryl Sandberg, former

Google executive, to Chief Operating Officer. The partnership added an additional aspect to Zuck's legacy, one in which other founders try to mimic. Instead of bringing in big-name execs to push their own agendas, entrepreneurs are seeking proven executives who will complement and support their visions.

Hack #4: Know what your users want better than they do. Facebook's user interface and system upgrades happen without notice, often and are constantly met with strong and vocal user resistance. Zuck doesn't seem to care. Case in point, in September 2006, with no prior heads up, FB introduced the News Feed. 700,000 users out of 9 million (almost 10% of all users) joined a group to protest the change. Zuck apologized in a blog post for the way FB communicated the update (or lack thereof), but continued to press forward. In this particular situation, Zuck believed he knew what his users wanted more than they did—and he was right. "When we launched the Status Update, the reaction from the outside world was, 'Why would anyone want to share some small snippet of what they are doing right now?' Well, no one is asking that anymore," Zuck said in a 2009 interview.

Another example of his foresight is in May 2007, when he realized the creative potential of the masses and made Facebook an open source platform, inviting programmers to code their own apps that could run on the social network. Through this single move, the platform birthed a storm of innovation. In the same year, Facebook added the "People you May Know" function, which algorithmically suggests new connections to users and helped contribute to Facebook doubling in size (to nearly 200 million users) that year.

Zuck has understood things even his users haven't, and if you look at almost every major, new feature update, you can trace some sort of resistance by members. It even happened with Facebook Connect—which allows FB members to log into other websites with the FB username and password—that started off as an advertising service called Beacon, and started off by making users rebel. However, equally impressive, is the fact that Zuck has been bold enough to push forward with updates, despite strong resistance by his user base and more often than not prove to them why they need whatever he prescribes.

Hack #5: Be a hacker CEO. "I think Mark Zuckerberg is 'the one'. Like Bill Gates and Steve Jobs, he has set a tone that everyone else has lined up behind," says Roger McNamee, venture capitalist and FB investor.

Zuck's true genius has always been to facilitate "The Hacker Way." It is the foundational ethos of Facebook. In its IPO prospectus, FB repeatedly describes its corporate culture as "The Hacker Way." At its Headquarters in Menlo Park, there is even a big sign that reads "The Hacker Company."

Every Zuckerberg hack is in the aid of his overarching vision: that technology and online authenticity can unite people in ways new even to the World Wide Web. Facebook's wild success and worldwide dominance is a testament to his unrivaled vision. Plus arguing with him seems to be a losing battle anyway.

Bloomberg BusinessWeek, May 2012, How Mark Zuckerberg Hacked the Valley. Brad Stone and Douglas MacMillan

REDDIT AND ALEXIS OHANIAN: MAKING THE WORLD SUCK LESS

Building the Front Page of the Internet was done in 2005, by Alexis Ohanian and Steve Huffman, who cofounded Reddit. Reddit was one of the first startups birthed from Paul Graham's renowned tech Launch Pad—Y Combinator. Sixteen months after its creation, the social-news site was acquired by Condé Nast—hurtling Ohanian into a new tax bracket, making him a 23-year-old multimillionaire.

In Ohanian's junior year in college, while taking the LSAT-Prep Course, he flipped over the test and thought, "you bastards." He says, "I walked out and went to the waffle house. That's where I had what I call The Waffle House Epiphany: I didn't want to be a lawyer. I wanted to make a dent in the Universe."

His college roommate had a dream to build a mobile food ordering business dubbed "mymobilemenu." Alexis spent his senior year researching the business, competition and planned to launch the company locally. During this time, the two boys heard Paul Graham was speaking in Boston and headed there from Virginia. Paul Graham ended up inviting them to interview for Y Combinator, which was relatively unknown around that time.

Ohanian explains, "The night of the interview, Paul called me and said, 'I'm sorry we're not accepting you.' That sucked. Really sucked. So we got drunk. Really drunk. The next morning, hungover, I get a call from Paul. He says, 'I'm sorry, we made a mistake. We don't like your idea, but we like you guys. You guys need to build the front page of the Internet.' That was all Paul, and that became Reddit."

Reddit was built in three weeks. The first version was just web links, text submitted by users and interesting or uninteresting buttons that users could click on, underneath the web links and text. Understanding that value was in the user base, the team agreed to add a comments section.

Sixteen months after its development, Condé Nast acquired Reddit for a reported $10 to $20 million. Paul Graham was ecstatic—not only was Reddit one of the first startups to launch in Y Combinator, but they were also the first significant acquisition. Ohanian says he's tithed since the day they sold Reddit and believes wealth is a means to an end he states, "I really believe my resources are best used to help projects that make the world suck less."

Since the sale of Reddit he's vowed to stay hungry; Ohanian has launched a social enterprise called "Breadpig" cofounded a travel-search site named "Hipmunk" and created an investment firm dubbed "Das Kapital Capital" that has placed capital in 25 startups. He says, "When I see business models disrupted from the outside, I am delighted. I see progress—progress!"

And, so far, in his young career, Ohanian has in fact, made the world suck less.

Inc. Magazine, June 2012, How I Did It. Christine Lagorio

JACK DORSEY: THE NEW STEVE JOBS?!

"Visionaries are that rare breed of people who have the insight to match an emerging technology to a strategic opportunity," states Geoffrey A. Moore in his classic book, "Crossing the Chasm."

Jack Dorsey, 35 (at the time of this writing), is often mentioned as the "one" to fill Steve Jobs' shoes in the pecking order of visionary tech entrepreneurs—and, has already masterminded not one but two of today's most innovative technology companies. In 2006, he invented Twitter which has since advanced from short-character focused social networking site into the *de facto* platform for real-time news (from politics, to sports, to entertainment). In 2009, he constructed Square, which originated as a credit card processing device that plugs into a smartphone's audio jack and has morphed into a mobile swipe-free payment app and an alternative to a cash register through the Square's tablet app.

Dorsey's visions springs from the theory that innovation happens when disparate thoughts mesh. "It's important to demystify the term. Innovation is just reinvention and rethinking. I don't think there's anything truly, organically new in this world. It's just mash-ups of all these things that provide different perspectives—that allow you to think in a completely different way, which allows you to work in a different way," states Dorsey.

Seth Stevenson, of the Wall Street Journal Magazine, writes with both Twitter and Square, Dorsey's flashes of insight are by-products of a lifelong quest for simplicity and order. Dorsey yearns to create streamlined beauty out of giant ungainly systems that at first glance appear to be irredeemably chaotic. He makes the impossible happen through efficiency of motion.

Twitter was born out of Dorsey's crazy teenage fixation of eavesdropping on radio chatter from local ambulances, when determined he could write a program that would make the dispatch process more efficient. He then found the largest dispatch company in the world, hacked its corporate servers, sent an e-mail to its CEOs' unlisted e-mail address explaining the breach and asking for a job, and then moved from St. Louis to NY to become its lead programmer—he did this all by age 18. Learning to streamline and organize this type of communication led to the epiphany of Twitter, which lets anyone, rather than just dispatchers, broadcast instant messages across the globe versus just across a city grid.

The existence of Square serves an entirely different industry, with Dorsey's signature disruptive nature at its core. The genesis of Square came when Dorsey's friend and mentor was explaining that he had just lost out on a $2,000 sale on one of his hand-blown glass pieces. His small shop couldn't justify the credit card merchant service fees, and the customer did not have cash on her. Dorsey says, "As I was commiserating with him over our cellphones, it occurred to me that we were both holding up to our ears very powerful general-purpose computers! I thought there must be some way we could use them to do easy money transfers."

And so began the birth of Square, a tiny device that Dorsey engineered which enables merchants to swipe credit cards that plugs right into the headphone jack of a smartphone. For small business owners and self-employed entrepreneurs, Square is heaven-sent: no upfront costs, simple to use, instant operability and complete mobility. Square has made it astoundingly effortless for anyone to be able to accept credit cards. Here's how it works: at no cost, square mails the device to anyone who requests it, the moment the recipient grabs the device from the mail, they plug it into a smartphone and can start accepting all major credit cards while being charged with a simple 2.75-percent fee for all transactions. The standard process for small businesses to accept credit cards is notoriously difficult and painstakingly slow; issuing banks require multiple proofs of credit worthiness and pile on extravagant fees. In addition to Square streamlining the payment process, they've added an additional layer of value through the business analytics it can now provide its merchant business partners—who's buying what, how much of it and how often. It doesn't stop there, with its two latest mobile and tablet applications, Square empowers consumers a swipe free payment option—the pay with Square app lets a customer who's just entered a store have the ability to make a purchase without swiping anything. The customer simply states his name, and the vendor's app confirms the transaction by locating any nearby smartphones running the app then uses the customer's photo as confirmation, before it processes the linked credit card information. "Our sign-up process takes literally two minutes. You download an app, put your name and address, answer three security questions, link your bank account, and you're done." Dorsey explains.

The second latest application is the Square Register which replaces the cash register with a table app, enabling merchants to use their tablet as the new cash drawer. The app connects via Wi-Fi and lets vendors set up buttons for each item in their store.

Dorsey says, "Face-to-face commerce today is socially impoverished. Human beings have been handling money for thousands of years, but it is still an awkward, time-consuming, unplugged, and uninspiring experience. What if it were beautiful?" Through Square, Dorsey is creating a solution to that simple question, and aims to create an emotionally appeasing experience for shoppers—with a page of simplicity and superior design, right out of the Apple Playbook. As Steven Levy of Wired says, the vision—swipeless pay, if you will—was a logical extension of turning payment into an intimate experience. And just like Jobs did, Dorsey works hand in hand with his design team. But perhaps Dorsey's most Jobsian trait is his knack for disrupting entire industries and forcing them to follow his lead, says Levy. Dorsey recognizes massive societal inefficiencies and strives to make them efficient, which is a more top down approach in contrast to Jobs' laser like product focus. "The best innovations come out of real problems and real pain," says Dorsey.

Yet, as one industry reporter puts it, Dorsey seems to have inherited Jobs' title as "the most fascinating man in tech." And like Jobs, through Dorsey's unique worldview perspective, genuinely eccentric character and seemingly God-given calling to change the world through tech, he has somewhat amassed a somewhat cult-like following. Dorsey has his hands full—in addition to his fulltime gig as CEO of Square, he maintains the post as Executive Chair of Twitter—and some big shoes to fill—being mentioned in the same breath as Jobs, but still, after reading about and studying Dorsey, it is apparent he wears those shoes well.

Wired Magazine, July 2012, The Many Sides of Jack Dorsey. Steven Levy
Wall Street Journal Magazine, October, 2012 Simplicity and Order for All. Seth Stevenson

DIY DRONES: MAKING IT
THE ERA OF THE PERSONAL DRONE

DIY drones now outnumber military drones in the U.S. (Wired Magazine, July 2012, Chris Anderson). The claim is that with cheap sensors, off-the-shelf parts, and free open-source software, now anybody can own a personal flying robot. A drone is defined as an aircraft that has autonomous flight, which means they can follow a mission from point to point (typically guided by GPS, but very soon this will also be done through vision and sensor helping drones to start "thinking for themselves").

In 2007, Chris Anderson (editor of Wired Magazine and source of this writing) registered diydrones.com and developed a social networking site for people tinkering with autonomous aircraft. As Chris Anderson explains, "More and more autopilot electronics look just like smartphone electronics simply running different software. The technical and economic advantages of coattailing on the economics of scale of the trillion-dollar mobile-phone industry are astounding. If you want to understand why the personal-drone revolution is happening now, look no further than your pocket."

Chris Anderson's social networking site has 26,000 plus (as of July 2012) members and says that there are around 1,000 DIY drones taking flight per month. In fact, the personal drone industry is growing more rapidly than the world's top aerospace companies (in units not dollars), the cause being equivalent to the advance of all digital technology: Moore's Law. Moore's Law being that power and performance of computer chips increase while price and size decrease. Anderson compares the acceleration of drone adoption to the 1970's birth and revolution of personal computers, and predicts this decade to be the rise of the personal drone.

Anderson teaches that the key component in a drone is the autopilot, which is a combination of a barometric-pressure meter, a compass, and mechanical gyroscopes (motorized flywheels with analog electrical outputs). Due to Moore's Law, today's sensors used to make an autopilot system are immensely smaller in size and drastically cheaper. The entire system—starting with gyroscopes (which measure rates of rotation), magnometers (used as a digital compass), pressure sensors (used to calculate altitude by measuring atmospheric pressure) and accelerometers (which measure the force of gravity)—and its capabilities can be found in a tiny chip, at your neighborhood RadioShack. The latest system comprises of all the necessary capabilities (nine sensors total), plus a temperature gauge and a processor, into one tiny package for as low as 17 bucks.

The brain of the autopilot, a single chip microprocessor, navigates the drone based on the information from sensors. Thanks to technological advancements in the smartphone industry, which necessitates tiny but massively powerful processing power and hyper-efficient battery life, these processors now dominate the single-chip industry and are instrumental in powering today's personal drones. Not just that, but these lightly power-efficient, capable chips empower drones to go beyond following commands and help the bots to start thinking for themselves.

It doesn't stop there, the smartphone technology goes further than just powering drones by microprocessors—the need for high quality cameras has propelled a comparable evolution in image-capturing capabilities, stronger GPS for phones has translated to drones, wireless radio modules, memory and batteries, are all, also contributing to the rise of the personal flying robot. As Anderson states, "In short, this new generation of cheap, small drones is essentially a fleet of flying smartphones."

At this stage, the DIY community is simply tinkering, twisting and experimenting with their drones. However, as the community becomes more intelligent and the technology more powerful and inexpensive, real world applications will arise. Already, law enforcement and government have found specific uses, the entertainment industry is saturated with flying bots serving as camera platforms, some farmers use them to map out optimal planting areas and for crop management, and there are endless scientific uses—from wildlife observation to weather analysis. With the majority of progress coming directly from the DIY drone movement, as Anderson exclaims, "It's safe to say that drones are the first technology in history where the toy industry and lobbyists are beating the military-industrial complex at its own game." And in terms of opportunity the personal flying drone movement represents, really sky's the limit.

Wired Magazine, July 2012, Here Come the Drones. Anderson

ERIC RIES AND THE LEAN STARTUP METHOD: THE STARTUP'S SAVIOR AND TECH SECTOR'S NEW TESTAMENT

Ries, in his early thirties is Silicon Valley's latest "it man." In the four years he started writing an anonymous blog about his gospel of replacing the traditional product development cycle, with an organized system based on experimentation, he has sparked a movement. The movement goes farther than just the 90,000 plus copies, his book, "The Lean Startup," sold, passed the 75,000 subscribers his blog attracts. It's bigger than even the fact that Harvard Business School has incorporated his principles into its entrepreneurship curriculum. The true measure that Ries' movement has landed on its intended destination is through the army of disciples his gospel has assembled, and the creation of their own books, events, websites, blogs, apps and businesses based on his teachings. Lean Startup slang has become so saturated that Techcrunch has banned the use of his term "pilot." Tech darlings like Groupon, Dropbox and Zappos lead as Lean Startup benchmarks, while the message has now started infiltrating established companies like Intuit and GE.

The power of the Lean Startup method lies in its core foundation, which is based on the scientific method; the business parallel to clinical trials. Ries states that every single business is based on a key set of assumptions and those assumptions must be tested rigorously. His commandments read: Test your ideas before you bet the bank on them. Don't listen to what focus groups say; watch what your customers do. Start with a modest product offering and build on the aspects of it that prove valuable with customers. Expect to fail, and stay flexible enough in your strategy to try again and again until you get it right.

Correct or incorrect, the Lean Startup is based on a relentless set of logic. Its message rings true to tech entrepreneurs of all types; from cynical startup vets still bruised from the Dotcom bust, to rookie tech entrepreneurs blessed with open source code caches and worldwide reach.

Ries had his epiphany while attending Steve Blank's Entrepreneurship course at UC Berkeley—a stipulation Steve Blank made with the founder of the startup Ries worked for at the time, for making an investment in the company. Blank explained that startups are not a smaller version of established companies, that neither the product nor the customers are known. The only solution is to put real features in front of customers, track their response, rinse, and repeat until the product gains traction. For Ries, the class was a game-changer (similar to my reading Ries' book). While CTO of IMVU (the startup Ries worked for), Ries cut his teeth with the approaches he learned from Blank. The next four years he spent fusing teachings from Blank's self-published startup handbook "The Four Steps to the Epiphany" with disciplines derived from Kent Beck's "Extreme Programming Explained," the lean manufacturing guide—"The Machine that Changed the World," and Geoffrey A. Moore's bible for entrepreneurial marketing "Crossing the Chasm." Powered by these innovative approaches, Eric Ries and IMVU, tested out-of-the-box ways to learn who its customers were and what they wanted.

An example of this practice in play was when he realized rather than spend time and energy coding a product, he could learn the same thing from a simple description of the product, and a "Download Now!" button (called a Minimum Viable Product—MVP). Using Google's AdWord program, to drive internet traffic at a low price, he spent $5 a day to attract 100 visitors. Ries navigated his visitors through different designs and collated the differences in their behavior (a practice named split or A/B testing). He tracked the shifting percentages in groups, as visitors registered, logged in, used the product and upgraded to the paid version (known as cohort analysis). And he updated code as frequently as 50 times a day (which he refers to as continuous deployment). Through these processes, and many failed attempts, IMVU prospered. And the Lean Startup method had its genesis.

It makes zero difference that the Lean Startup method is a collection of ideas culled from coding, manufacturing, marketing and business strategy substantiated with real world insights that have been passed around the Silicon Valley elite for years. Ries does not hide his sources, and his pitch preempts critics' complaints. "Lean." he explains, "does not mean cheap; it means eliminating waste by testing ideas first and it doesn't mean small, but rather that companies shouldn't ramp up personnel and facilities until they've validated their business model."

Eric Ries defines a startup as an organization dedicated to creating something new under conditions of extreme uncertainty. This is just as true for one person in a garage as it is in a group of seasoned professionals in a Fortune 500 boardroom. What they all have in common is a mission to penetrate the fog of uncertainty to discover a successful path to a sustainable business. If classic authors and entrepreneurs like Geoffrey A. Moore, Steve Blank and Clayton M. Christensen are Old Testament prophets, then Ries is the startup savior, and those of us applying his gospel have inadvertently rose to discipleship. Most startups fail. But many of those failures are preventable and the New Testament Lean Startup method becomes the only saving grace.

Wired Magazine, June 2012, The Upstart. Ted Greenwald
The Lean Startup. 2012, Eric Ries Crown Business Publishing

KURT VARNER: AND HIS VERSION
OF THE LEAN STARTUP METHOD

Meet Kurt Varner. Kurt is 25 years old. Kurt is a tech entrepreneur. Kurt is launching his business in Silicon Valley. And Kurt is living in his car.

Varner is very much the prototypical entrepreneur. He left his high paying position as a flight-test engineer, at Edwards Air Force Base in L.A., to pursue something he was passionate about. So he took the entrepreneurial plunge.

His first business was a video-blogging site, that didn't lead anywhere. After getting boxed out by larger competitors on his next venture, he vowed to do things right—he'd obtain a technical cofounder, a network of mentors and connections, a little seed capital, and he would do it all in the right place—launch in the Valley.

Just one issue: his wife teaches 3rd grade and she could not leave her job mid-year. Paying rent on two apartments was out of the question and waiting four months—to relocate—"The word wait should not be in the entrepreneur's vocabulary," Varner states. So he packed a duffle bag and headed north.

Not surprisingly enough, his newfound hunger, mental focus and positive impatience stems from the fact that he just completed Eric Ries' book, "The Lean Startup." Maybe taking the title a little too literal, his priorities since arriving in the Valley is to create a network of advisers, influencers and potential partners.

Varner's ambition and desire cannot be mistaken, but his approach to launching his venture seems to be missing the mark. Brian Wong, founder of Kiip (a company that allows game developers to reward players with real goods) picked up on the fact after taking a meeting with him while offering his own advice. Wong says, "Stop asking people for advice, you've had enough meetings."

Wong urges Varner to make a video illustrating his concept, and launch it on Kickstarter to attract funding. Wong even insists that he would provide the first $100 to get started. Wong must have read The Lean Startup himself, because launching a minimum viable product is a page right out of Eric Ries' Playbook. The Lean Startup method does not mean cheap; it means eliminating waste by testing ideas first. And it definitely doesn't say anything about sleeping in your car. Although I do appreciate and respect the do-whatever-it-takes entrepreneurship attitude Varner shows, and truly hope he finds success.

Inc. Magazine, July/August 2012, The Leanest Startup. Leigh Buchanan

FINANCE STRATEGY: NAVIGATING THE TERM SHEET

First and foremost, just because you receive a term sheet, does not guarantee funding. Obviously, receiving a term sheet is reason for small celebration but not the actual touchdown dance—more like the high steppin' ball in front of body maneuver on your way to the end zone. But anything can happen on your way to 6 points, and in the fundraising game, most likely will.

There are a number of areas that frequently become points of negotiation between entrepreneurs and investors, which we'll expose. And yes, a term sheet is on the path to getting funded, but strings come attached, and it can also represent a way for investors to gain control of your board and dilute your shares. Term sheets are also nonbinding, and you'll want to consult a securities lawyer to support in the negotiation process and in translating what the term sheet actually spell out.

Point #1: Valuation is typically the first place a negotiation with an investor will start. It's essentially an agreement with investors about how much the company is worth. In other words, how much equity you will give away, for how much money you will receive. The valuation of an early stage company is sometimes difficult to determine because an early stage venture typically is not generating revenues or profits. So, numerous other variables help set the valuation. Variables like industry comparables (an established company doing something similar to yours, that has revenues that you can compare your venture to), market size, unique intellectual property of patents, the strength and experience of the founding team and any other information you can provide that substantiates your valuation. The reason you hear determining a valuation is an art, not science is because there is no exact formula for setting a price on a company with no revenues. Although, professional investors typically know what they like to see in a startup they invest in, and doing your due diligence on your investors will prove invaluable. It is also critical to understand the difference between "premoney" and "postmoney" valuation—the value of the company before and after the investment. For example, say a company will have a postmoney valuation of $10 million, which includes $2 million from investors. That means the premoney valuation is $8 million. The greater the premoney valuation in relation to the postmoney valuation, the more of the company the founders get to keep. Keep in mind, the valuation can be used as a negotiation tactic, and rather than squabble with investors over a couple dollars (assuming the disparity of your valuation and expectations, and theirs, are not too far apart), give them their valuation while you negotiate another point. For instance, yes Mr. Investor I'll agree to your premoney valuation of $7,850,000 rather than our $8 million, if you'll agree to a two year vesting schedule versus the three year proposed in the term sheet or whatever term sheet point means more to you and your team. Just remember, whatever valuation you set, make sure you can show logically (key word) with as much proof and facts how you came up with that number.

Point #2: Vesting plans are put in place so that if an investor invests into the company, the founders can't simply walk away from the business and keep their shares. It is also a way for founders to keep other founders and early employees around too. A vesting plan states that founders and any other common shareholders (excluding investors who are typically preferred shareholders) are required to earn their ownership shares over a certain time frame, usually two to three years. Case in point, Founder A is to receive 30% ownership and agrees to a three year vesting schedule. He could receive 10 percent equity, every year, for three years, or however other way the vesting plan is structured. Because founders own 100 percent of the shares before they bring on investors, agreeing to a vesting schedule can be confusing at first, but it is standard for the industry and is helpful in providing a sense of longer term stability for the company.

Point #3: Stock option pools are created as a reserve to compensate future employees, and most term sheets include them. A habitual area of contention is whether the size of the pool is created before premoney or postmoney valuation is set. When the option pool comes out of premoney, the founders' shares are diluted.

Point #4: Board control is a very important issue. Making sure you have proper representation on the board is vital. A common term sheet may state that investors get two seats, the common shareholders get two, and a fifth goes to an agreed-upon 3rd party, like an industry expert. When determining who will fill the two seats for the common shareholders it is best to leave room for yourself and a CEO because not all founders remain CEOs postmoney.

Point #5: Antidilution protection prevents an investor's equity stake from being diluted by later investments. If investors suspect that one round of funding won't suffice, they will most likely attempt to secure aggressive antidilution provisions. The most aggressive being a provision called a "full ratchet." A full ratchet allows the investors to maintain the same ownership percentage in the company even if the company takes on future funding, with the future equity diluting the founders' shares. Fortunately, most investors agree to a weighted average antidilution term that weighs the value of the investors' money based on when it was invested, which tends to offer protection to the founder's equity.

Point #6: Dividend requests are standard in term sheets and investors typically request an annual 8 percent dividend, but that money is rarely pulled out of the startup because the company is usually not yet profitable and it is wiser to reinvest the money back into the company. One thing to look out for is if the term sheet states that dividends are cumulative, which means dividends compound year after year, and can be expensive for a company that doesn't sell or go public for four or five years down the road.

Point #7: Liquidation preference explains how founders and investors will be paid after a sale or IPO, and can be another sticky point of negotiation. Investors almost always request preferred shares, versus the common shares retained by founders and employees, and preferred shareholders typically get paid first when everyone cashes out. "Participating preferred" shareholders also share in payouts that would otherwise be given to common stockholders, which can be an issue if no cap is set on the payout the participating preferred shareholders receive. For example, if the term sheet states that investors would receive uncapped participating preferred stock, then they would be entitled to two sources of cash if the company is sold. First, most term sheets have a clause in the liquidation section that guarantees the investor x amount times its original investment (the x depends on the space, investment climate and other variables), plus any accumulated dividends. Second, because the investor has equity ownership, they receive the percentage of their ownership on monies left over to payout common stockholders. In a perfect world, there will be some sort of cap, and if not, a cap makes for a strong negotiation point.

Point #8: "No-shop" provisions are often tucked away at the end of term sheets, which specifies that upon signing the term sheet, an entrepreneur will stop the process of courting other investors. Most investors will push for 60 to 90 days, which is too long, and asking for 30 days is a better strategy.

Negotiating the term sheet is a skillful game of tug-and-war. It is chess not checkers. Congratulations to you for receiving a term sheet. Realize that this is the first step, and some investors will do whatever it takes to negotiate in their favor, but none of it matters until the money is in the bank. None of it.

Engineering Your Start-up, 2003, James A. Swanson and Michael L. Baird. PPI Professional Series

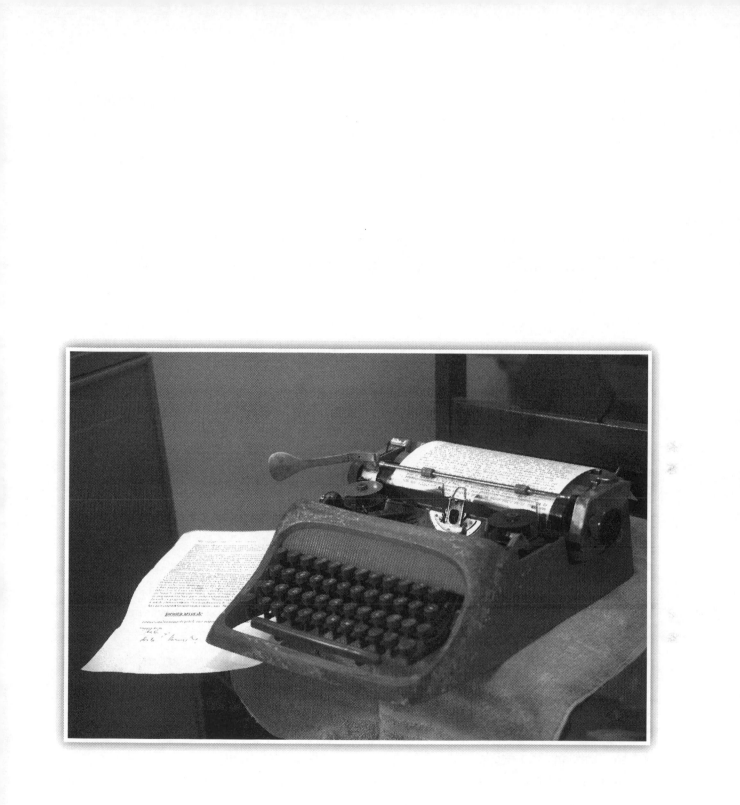

THE DRAPER DYNASTY:
SILICON VALLEY'S CONTRADICTION

"Silicon Valley is much more of a meritocracy than traditional lines of business. Has the founder of any major tech company, been the son or daughter of another tech entrepreneur? Change favors the entrant," says Steve Jurvetson, partner of Draper Fisher Jurvetson, a Silicon Valley venture capital fund. The valley is not known for respecting the silver spooner trappings of old money, connections or inherited power. In fact, the opposite holds true, that the Valley is the last frontier to live the American Dream: a place where it doesn't matter who your parents are, where you went to college, or if you even dropped out for that matter—as long as you're willing to take a risk and pursue your dreams, you can make it. The Valley sees itself as a meritocracy, and yet smacks dab in the middle of it all is the Draper family. The Draper family is an anomaly.

The Draper dynasty extends back four generations to General William H. Draper Jr., a former undersecretary of the U.S. Army who is considered the first professional venture capitalist on the West Coast. It was 1958 and the General founded the firm Draper, Gaither & Anderson. He then recruited his son Bill, as one of the first employees, starting the Draper dynasty. "We rented a car and went out and knocked on doors in the orchards," says Bill talking about the groves that filled Sunnyvale. In those days, while working for his father, Bill says he would pull over to any storefront that had the word "technology" in its name, and ask the company if it needed financial support in exchange for equity.

In the 60's Bill started two VC funds—Draper & Johnson and Sutter Hill Ventures, and pioneered the mantra to invest in people rather than ideas. Bill became the second generation Draper, and placed capital in more than 500 companies, visited hundreds of countries and was the first VC to invest in emerging markets like India. Bill started in the venture capital game when deals were done with a handshake, and has had a tremendously successful, six-decade career, that encompasses money, politics and philanthropy. Bill has framed photos of himself with the elite network he fostered over his career, including U.S. presidents (George W. Bush, Clinton, Obama and Reagan), presidential runners (McCain and Romney), and even

Fidel Castro. Bill was vital in evolving venture capital into a respectable business, and is now a living patriarch of Silicon Valley.

Tim, Bill's son, and third generation Draper, believes his life's mission is to evangelize for venture capital. In the early 1980's Tim was trying to figure out his place in the world. He had a degree from Stanford and a degree from Harvard, but didn't know what to do next. "Eric Schmidt (of Google) was just a buddy and we were kind of looking at each other going, 'I don't know, what are you going to do?' Bill Gates was just getting going; Microsoft was a little private company. Steve Ballmer and Scott McNealy (of Sun Microsystems), you just ran into them," Tim reflects.

His path became clear when his father, Bill, was asked to run the import-export bank for the U.S. government. Before leaving for Washington, Bill handed Tim the keys to the family business. "Dad just set out a huge path for me, and all I had to do was go drive on it," Tim says.

Eventually, by the mid 2000's, Bill decided to found his own fund, and Draper Fisher Jurvetson was born. His firm rose to prominence with successful investments in Hotmail, Skype, Baidu and Tesla Motors. Through his success, Tim has become the most renowned member of the Draper crew—a billionaire partner at Draper Fisher Jurvetson. Today, the DFJ network has worldwide reach with 30 offices around the globe—from South Korea to Russia. He has a foundation to teach elementary and middle school student's entrepreneurship, and is launching Draper University, a program for 18-to-24 year olds. His next mission is to turn Silicon Valley into a state. "I've already written a constitution," he explains.

And now, the fourth generation Draper unit is ready to embark on its Silicon Valley journey. Three of Tim's four children—Jesse, Adam and Billy—are entering the startup world, with Silicon Valley breeding running through their veins. "We've just been raised with anything is possible mentality," says Billy, Tim's youngest son. Each kid is dabbling in different industries—Jesse in media, Adam finance and Billy marketing: yet, despite the Draper bloodline, there is no guarantee that this generation of Drapers can continue the family dynasty. And, that is the beauty of meritocracy, you are defined by what you accomplish, not what you were given although their inheritance of connections, wealth and relentless optimism will prove useful in the startup game and especially prominent industries-at-the-ready component of the Draper connections. "I chase Billy down once a week, saying, 'Is it ready, is it ready?' I want to invest and be in on it [Billy's startup] from inception," says M.C. Hammer. "The Drapers are historically known throughout the Valley. If you've heard of venture capital, you've heard of the Drapers." The ex-rapper met Tim a decade ago, at the house of another elite Silicon Valley VC—Ron Conway.

But the road is long and unlike previous Draper generations past, this generation will be competing in a more mature industry with much lower barriers to entry, where startups are commonplace, where the VC industry is shifting and new funding sources are being uncovered daily. Plus, the widespread feeling among the Valley is that the DRJ is at the bottom end of top-tier firms, a once-great operation that has lost its fight. So, despite their lineage, this Draper generation is not guaranteed victory. And maybe that's what they need—a reason to battle, a call to something greater to continue passing the torch of something bigger than themselves. The Draper dynasty runs deep, and it sure would be a loss to see it fail, and I'd like to believe, even with all the odds against them, this generation—my generation—will have what it takes to continue its reign. They are simply, "too legit to quit," to quote another, well known Draper family friend.

Fast Company Magazine, July 2012, The Drapers of Silicon Valley. Danielle Sacks

ISRAELI RESERVE OFFICER, YARON GALAI: GETTING FUNDED WHILE UNDER FIRE

You think the fundraising road has been tough for you? Check out this cool story about Yaron Galai, CEO of Outbrain, as told in to Inc.'s J.J. McCorvey in their July/August 2012 issue. Outbrain, a New York City-based link recommendation platform for online publishers, is Yaron Galai's fourth company. He founded the first three in his native Israel, where he was a reserve officer, which makes for a great segway into his story:

Yaron Galai explains, "I was running a company called "Quigo," and I was called in to the reserve the last week of closing a $6 million investment deal. I thought it was too much information to tell the investors, so I took a cellphone to the naval base and kept negotiating the deal. When we got to the very last day of closing, we decided to get 25 people on a conference call. Fifteen minutes into the call, shooting starts around me."

He goes on, "That's just part of the fabric in Israel. Every man can be called to the reserve service for one month a year until the age of 45. The investors said they couldn't invest where the founders of the company were under fire. So I went into blatant begging mode. They offered a single new term: relocate to the United States within 45 days, and you can keep the investment. If by the 45th day we were not U.S. residents, we'd lose all equity in the company. Everything we had built, we would lose, and they would get it. Without that funding we would have had to shut down."

He exclaims, "On the spot, without talking to my wife or negotiating anything, I said 'It's a deal! Add it in there!' We literally moved on the 44th day, with our newborn son, Yuval. We sold Quigo to AOL for $340 million. But the reserve service is still something I deal with."

So, just remember the next time you start to complain about how difficult the fundraising road has been or how tough the climate seems—at least you're not getting shot at while fundraising.

Inc. Magazine, July/August 2012, Don't Shoot! I'm Getting Funded! J.J. McCorvey

LINKEDIN: SHOWING THE WORLD HOW A SOCIAL MEDIA COMPANY SHOULD BE RUN

Facebook, and its May IPO, has all the attention, but LinkedIn is quietly establishing its presence, along with a big pile of cash. LinkedIn makes its money by three ways; the first is marketing and advertising, the second, subscriptions by members, and the third, which is the richest and fastest growing opportunity, is selling member profiles to corporate recruiters.

Let's compare the two social media giants to better understand their businesses. First, LinkedIn's share price lagged Facebook's private-market gains, but has stayed ahead now that both are public (based on financial information from July 2012). Thanks to comScore's web-usage data and public company filings, we can now break down how much revenue each site captures for every hour each user spends on the platform. Here's the math.

Facebook: In July 2012, FB had 900,000,000 total members; multiply that by 6.35 (the Aug. monthly hours members spend on the site) and your total monthly hours per member is 5,715,000,000. Now take the monthly revenue ($352,670,000) and divide that by total member hours per month (5,715,000,000) and you get: 6.2 cents of hourly member revenue.

LinkedIn: In July 2012, LinkedIn had 161,000,000 total members, multiply that by 0.30 (the Aug. monthly hours spent on the site) and your total monthly hours per member is 48,300,000. Now take the monthly revenue ($62,818,000) and divide that by total member hours per month (48,300,000) and you get: $1.30 of hourly member revenue. *financial info provided by Forbes July, 2012*

Obviously, the argument can be that it is better to own a small slice of something huge, than a huge slice of something small, but that argument is further trumped by a simple fact: Facebook, who earns 85 percent of its revenue from advertising, makes money only when a user is on Facebook; and LinkedIn monetizes user information, earning revenues even when users are not on the site. Further, on average, Facebook users click on only one of every 2,000 ads, making it a moot point that FB users, on average, spend 6.35 hours per month on the site versus LinkedIn's 18 minutes. Plus, these variables will be even more intensified as the web goes mobile, because it is difficult to deliver ads to smartphones and tablets. At LinkedIn, where 22 percent of visits come from mobile devices, versus 8 percent a year ago, this increase simply equates to more opportunity, interactions and data it can earn revenues through unlike Google and FB where mobile means obstacles.

In 2003, Reid Hoffman cofounded LinkedIn, after PayPal was sold, where he was one of its earliest executives. He built the site on the assumption that getting lots of professionals connected in an online network was bound to be helpful, somehow. "We learned [from PayPal] that you could revolutionize an industry with people who are very smart, working hard and deploying a technology never seen before," Hoffman says.

Hoffman's assumption was validated by 2004, when LinkedIn hit 1 million members by word of mouth only. As LinkedIn's membership exploded past 20 million in 2008, a sustainable business model began to form. That year, Hoffman hired Yahoo veteran Jeff Weiner to take over as CEO.

Weiner started his career at Warner Bros., before joining Yahoo in 2001. He started in corporate development, but ended up running Yahoo's most important assets—Mail, Search, Sports and News. Rather than mimic Yahoo's mistakes of spreading itself too thin, Weiner enforced his LinkedIn strategy around getting the simple stuff right—making sure the site doesn't crash as often, running A/B tests to make sure they know what customers wanted, letting the data provide the solution and sell, sell, sell.

Weiner refined Hoffman's original assumption into a powerful, concise mantra: "connecting talent and opportunity at a massive scale." The maxim led LinkedIn into its victorious IPO in May 2011. After the IPO, Hoffman remained LinkedIn's largest shareholder, with an 18 percent stake valued at roughly $1.8 billion and is still the Executive Chairman even though most of his time is spent at Greylock partners where he's an active VC.

Weiner, controls $300 million in stock even after dumping 18 percent of his shares, and has been given the mission to continue building out the LinkedIn platform. Under Weiner's regime, the company has developed a sales centric culture and adds two new users per second. Three and a half years before Weiner joined LinkedIn, the company was running a $4.5 million annual loss. In July 2012, LinkedIn shares were up by 64 percent and was on track to gross $895 million and net $70 million, up 71 percent and 100 percent respectively, from 2011. Weiner has proven his value has generated wildly impressive numbers and has a grand, clear vision for the future of his company that would make any CEO jealous. With all of his success, he may even be able to teach that other social media CEO a thing or two.

Forbes Magazine, July 2012, The Other Social Network. George Anders

FACEBOOK: THE MODERN DAY TULIP

It's safe to say Facebook owned the year 2012, which was a mix of good and bad. The first half of the year marked great hype, anticipation and excitement for the world's largest internet company initial public offering. Zuck and Facebook could do no wrong, and investors couldn't wait to make the long-term bet that he was constructing something even bigger than Google. Investors saw limitless opportunity as the social media juggernaut quickly approached a billion users. As Brad Stone put it in a Bloomberg BusinessWeek article, "The Facebook proverbial glass wasn't half full, it was overflowing."

Then May came, and during the week of its offering, FB decided to add shares and increase the starting price to $38, which could have simply been a logical way to maximize the funds raised in its IPO. Pair that with subsequent technical problems during its first day of trading on the NASDAQ, and in a blink, Facebook became the modern day tulip. In an instant it became a symbol of frenzy and irrational impulse-buying. And, all of a sudden, talks of a bubble started surfacing.

Since its first day peak of $45 a share, the price has crumbled to around $20 (as of August 2012 financial information), which makes for a roughly 54 percent share decrease. The company's clear reported challenges have been magnified into impossible obstacles, things like the issue of figuring out how to monetize mobile, that several million accounts are either duplicates, businesses, software bots or even pets, top executives have left and announcement about its advertising growth slowing. Even good news has been negatively translated, like when Facebook met Wall Street's expectations in July 2012 and showed a 22 percent revenue increase—results that should have pleased investors—its stock price lost another 10 percent.

The public's perception of Facebook has been more volatile than reviews of The Social Network movie, and investors' buyer's remorse is as irrational as their pre-IPO euphoria. In the post-Facebook IPO environment, fear compounds fear, even when the company shows continued growth.

Bloomberg BusinessWeek, August 2012, The Facebook Freakout. Brad Stone

FACEBOOK: THE TIMELINE TRIBUTE FOR ITS 1 BILLIONTH USER

Even in the wake of its IPO ups and downs, the Facebook engine has continued to chug along without being derailed from its core mission, to make the world a more connected place.

September 14, 2012, what took the World Wide Web 30 or 50 years to accomplish, it took Facebook 8—the social media behemoth hit its 1 billionth user, one-seventh of the world's population and nearly half of the Internet's 2 billion plus user base. The outbreak of the Facebook epidemic has seemed like an almost effortless contagion. However, since 2007, the company has relied on a focused unit tasked with attracting new members to Facebook. A special ops type team, that has access to every area of Facebook's business, has had explosive growth from an original founding team of five to more than 150 soldiers.

In tribute to Facebook's 1 billion users, here is a timeline of the history of Facebook created by Ashlee Vance of Bloomberg BusinessWeek: Zuckerberg registers "thefacebook.com" and launches the site in February 2004. By June, Facebook receives its first investment from Peter Thiel for $500,000. Sean Parker of Napster fame becomes President, and by the end of the year they reach 1 million users. A few months after, News Corp. acquires MySpace. In July 2005, Facebook adds high school and international school networks and drops the "the" from facebook.com. In 2006, two years after launching, Facebook has become the seventh most heavily trafficked site on the internet according to comScore. In the fall, it opens registration so that an invitation is no longer required; anyone can join, and Facebook membership reaches 12 million by the end of the year. Later on in 2007, Microsoft announces it has purchased a 1.6% share of Facebook for $240, giving Facebook a $15 billion valuation. By April 2008, Facebook overtakes MySpace for unique visitors. Facebook has launched in German, Spanish and French. Dustin Moskowitz and much of the original Facebook team start to depart. In February 2009, Facebook introduces the "Like" button (there have been 113 trillion "Likes" since). In December, the new OAD declares the Word of the Year to be "unfriend." 2010 starts construction on a hyper efficient data center in Prineville, Ore. Meanwhile, "The Social Network," an unflattering portrait of Zuckerberg and his relationship with early colleagues, opens in theatres. Wins three Oscars. Zuckerberg declares he will study Chinese everyday for a year. In 2011, Zuckerberg vows to eat only meat from animals he slaughters himself. In 2012, Zuckerberg changes his relationship status to "married" along with new bride Priscilla Chan. Facebook IPOs at an initial price of $38 a share and quickly loses more than half of its value. What's in store for the future of Facebook and Zuck, only time will tell.

Bloomberg BusinessWeek July/August 2012, Chasing Facebook's Next Billion Users. Douglas Macmillan

CHAMATH PALIHAPITIYA AND SOCIAL + CAPITAL: SUPERHERO INVESTING

Social + Capital (the + is silent) is an elite gang of programmer entrepreneurs who've amassed vast riches together, and now invest, socialize and determine what to do with their fortunes together. The team is "interested in hard-core people doing hard-core things," whose roster of investors includes some of the biggest names in Silicon Valley.

Chamath Palihapitiya, 35 (in 2012), is already a decorated Silicon Valley vet, and had a very successful tenure while at Facebook. According to Zuck, it was in fact Palihapitiya who, in 2008, came to him and argued that Facebook needed a team dedicated to finding users. "He had this epiphany that by far the most important thing we had to do was just accelerate the rate at which people were signing up," Zuckerberg states.

He led the FB growth team and his value was easily apparent: when he started, the site had 50 million users, and when he left, it had 750 million. His stock in Facebook made him a centi-millionaire several times over, and he plans to continue making millions, if not billions through investments that serve high ideals. And so, in assembling Social + Capital, he had to seek courageous, purpose-driven characters to match his funds' crusading ambitions. What Palihapitiya was able to accomplish reads like a who's who of Silicon Valley—billionaires like Germany's Nicholas Berggruen, Hong Kong's Li Ka-Shing, Brazil's Jorge Paulo Lemann, and our own Eli Broad because he was impressed with their philanthropy focus. He recruited venture capitalists such as Peter Thiel, John Doerr, David Bonderman, a private equity investor, and Chase Coleman of hedge fund Tiger Global Management due to their success as professional investors. He enlisted entrepreneur technology mavens and visionaries like Reid Hoffman (LinkedIn), Sean Parker (Napster, Facebook), Kevin Rose (Digg), and Joe Hewitt (Mozilla Foundation, Facebook) to mentor and support entrepreneurs they invest in, because everyone has superpowers that are subtly different. Palihapitiya also set up corporate investors such as Facebook and the Mayo Clinic because of their gigantic checkbooks.

Palihapitiya grew up poor, in Canada, after his family fled Sri Lanka, due to his father's position as an official. He had made enemies because of his outspokenness about needless violence. They lived in a two-bedroom apartment—his parents slept in one bedroom, his two sisters in another, and he in the living room on a mattress he kept stored in a closet. He used to dream about being on the Forbes list, and the moment he heard about Silicon Valley, he fell in love. And his infatuation was based on the opportunity to create vast wealth, which he believes is a means to an end in creating social impact. He argues, "That the kind of companies that can help the most people and solve the most intractable problems can't help but be lucrative, that doing good while doing well isn't just possible, it's tautological. If you focus on impact, you will make money."

He has put his money where his mouth is, and of the $275 million Social + Capital has under management; $60 million is of his own—compared to traditional funds where founders have typically very little skin in the game. Talking about his superhero team and gathering everyone for a meeting of the minds, he says, "All of these interesting people having a day to thoughtfully engage in the big structural trends of our times and think of ways we can change things. That's just awesome. It's just really good." And I can't help but agree.

Bloomberg BusinessWeek, July/August 2012, The League of Extraordinarily Rich Gentlemen. Drake Bennet

NICK SWINMURN AND ZAPPOS: TONY WHO?

When you hear the name Zappos, you can't help but think Tony Hsieh. I mean, he is the founder, right? Wrong. Nick Swinmurn came up with the idea after solving a personal problem, and persuaded Hsieh to invest. Here's Nick's and the Zappos story: he was at the mall one day looking for a specific pair of Airwalks and couldn't find them. So he thought, why not do an online store? He went to Footwear etc. in Sunnyvale, CA and told them, "I'll take some pictures, put your shoes online, and if people buy them, I'll buy them from you at full price."

The store agreed, and he received a few orders. It was 1999; he raised $150,000 and quit his day job to focus on the business full time. The business model stayed the same—go into stores, take pictures and sell the shoes online. In an effort to create something fun and different, he took the Spanish word "zapatos," added a "p" and came up with "Zappos."

He started taking meetings with VCs, but nobody thought people would buy shoes without trying them on first, and was getting turned down a lot. Around that time, his attorney Art Schneiderman introduced him to some guys that would invest in anything.

Enter Tony Hsieh and his team called Venture Frogs. Hsieh had just sold his company LinkExchange to Microsoft for $295 million in 1998, and was enthusiastic about investing. He put up $500,000 initially and joined the Zappos team. In 2001, they became co-CEOs and Tony put up $15 million of his personal cash into the company. They owned a dozen apartments in San Francisco and kept selling them to keep Zappos open. It was an uphill battle the next couple years, but were close to breaking even by 2003 and growing quickly. Sales for 2003 were $70 million, $184 million in 2004, and $370 million in 2005, and $597 million by 2006.

However, by 2006, Nick was getting bored. He recalls, "I wanted to be in the trenches with a small company again, so I decided to leave. I left him with all my stock and still retained ownership in the company.'

In 2009, his proposed solution to find the Airwalks he wanted by selling shoes online, was handsomely rewarded when Amazon purchased Zappos for $1.2 billion. He has been dubbed the "silent founder," but if money talks—now, he's shouting.

Fortune Magazine, September 2012, Zappos' Silent Founder. Dinah Eng

THE ERA OF ALGORITHM: DOING WHAT WE DO BETTER

Ashlee Vance of Bloomberg BusinessWeek tells us that, "Algorithms have been around since the ninth century Persian mathematician Abu Abdullah Muhammad ibn Musa al-Khwarizmi coined the term in a seminal mathematics text. But it's only in the last 20 years or so that we've really seen the uses of the algorithm explode and the concepts itself become fetishized. This is the result of the immense amount of cheap computing power now available and our ability to gather and store data on an unprecedented scale. We built algorithm machines—computer chips that speak 'if this, then that' in 1s and 0s—and can now feed them."

An algorithm is simply a mathematical formula used to solve a problem. And that problem can be anything—Vance says there are algorithms for picking music hits, actually composing music symphonies that sound as if a human composer created it, how much a movie will gross, reviewing legal documents better than professional law-dogs and algorithms that support the medical community by being able to accurately spot cancerous tumors.

Wall Street was the first industry to capture the power of the algorithm, where traders designed algorithms to find disparities in the market and solved the problem by creating algorithms that automatically executed buy and sell trades. In the not so distant past, (say the 80's), algorithmic-high-frequency trades were still the minority, as compared to today where computer based trades make up the majority of the trading floor. In fact, algorithm based trading has been so effective and competitive it has carved a new industry segment into Wall Street. "Quants" are comprised of scientists, physicists, statisticians, engineers and mathematicians whose sole mission is to create more powerful algorithms than their competitors, helping put to rest the argument that algorithms will basically control every aspect of our lives, that humans and our thoughts will be made obsolete. It's the same dispute critics of artificial intelligence make. Granted, algorithms and robotics will replace some tasks—it will be jobs they can do better than humans, and new industries will arise that will require the human touch, segments we may not even be able to envision yet. For instance, in the early days of Wall Street, nobody knew what a "quant" was.

So, rather than fight the advancing technology, I propose we embrace it and figure out how to best apply it like some companies have for example, Facebook has an algorithm that suggests people to befriend based on a number of different variables (where you went to school, where you work and live, who you are already friends with, etc.) and another algorithm called EdgeRank that determines what should show up in your newsfeed. Vance explains that sites like Zynga use algorithms to cogent people into playing games online longer and Uber's algorithm-based reservation system has created an on-demand car service, where wasted time previously existed. And just imagine the endless possibilities of algorithms we can use for good once we truly harness their capabilities—we could figure out what regions have food shortages and surpluses to feed the hungry, what if we could somehow use algorithms to mathematically negotiate world peace and prevent natural disasters. Algorithms have already proved their value, and the only limit they have are the limits we put on them. I think it's time to get excited about algorithms, to see how they will alter our future and to see in what ways they will support our existence.

Bloomberg BusinessWeek, September 2012, The End of Free Will. Ashlee Vance

COURSERA:
THE FUTURE OF HIGHER EDUCATION

The need to update and enhance our higher education system has been apparent for years now. More importantly with the advent of social media, the increasing power of computing and overall technological advancement, the climate to disrupt has never before been more ripe. And disruption is what has been happening—in the past year, a multitude of high profiled online course ventures have sprung up. The startups each boast of professors from elite universities teaching online courses for free. Most have social–media and video applications, all have attracted millions in venture funding, and most notable, all have enrollments of at minimum six figures. The main programs, currently (September 2012) are EDX, Minerva Project, Udacity and Coursera which all offer higher learning programs at no cost (except for the Minerva Project which charges $20,000 a year for tuition).

Coursera became the brainchild of ex-Stanford professors Andrew Ng and Daphne Koller, who have been friends for 13 plus years, when Koller became interested in how artificial intelligence could be used to improve student engagement, simultaneous to Ng building a software platform for online courses. They decided to marry the two in order to personalize learning and lower its cost of delivery.

In April 2012, the two launched their startup—Coursera—with $16 million of prominent venture backing from John Doerr at Kleiner Perkins Caulfield & Byers and Scott Sandell at New Enterprise Associates. The Coursera vision is clear and magnificent: to teach millions of people around the world for free, while also transforming how top universities teach.

Coursera courses are 6 to 10 weeks long with an hour or two of lecture videos per week. The videos are broken into short pieces and interactive engagement is added so that every 5 minutes there is a question. Ng and Koller have derived this type of learning from neuroscience research that states, "learning in instant retrieval," has led to enhanced memory versus the, "traditional end of chapter" study questions. In addition to the pop questions, the courses include weekly exercises, which encompass anything from problem sets, to design projects, essays, even a final project or test. For all quantitative courses, the platform uses artificial intelligence to evaluate each longer exercise, with real-time results. Students can keep trying until they get the problem correct. Leaving thousands of other students taking the course at the same time has tremendous advantages. Students can help each other in the Coursera forums, where study groups emerge assembled by class, language and time zone. Ng's first class he taught on machine learning, drew 104,000 eager students around the world (each class they had offered initially—machine learning, artificial intelligence and programming—had attracted more than 100,000 enrollments). Ng was astonished. "It would take me 250 years to teach this many people at Stanford," he states.

Besides the apparent manifest function of online education—teaching students that particular subject—a less obvious and maybe more impressive latent function is the fact that it can give academia a deeper understanding as to the way people actually learn. Through the sheer data Coursera courses generate—every single click, pause, rewind, the number of attempts to get a problem right, and what each student did in between—it creates an opportunity to improve the teaching and learning process. The average classroom has 20 students; the big ones have 200. Koller explains, "Here we have 20,000 or even 200,000, and it just completely changes your ability to extract meaningful conclusions from the data. It is an unprecedented opportunity to understand human learning."

Online education is not new unto itself, for the past 10 years people have had the ability to view lectures online from top professors, at elite universities, and dabble in course work and problem solving on their own time. However, the experience has been merely static, as compared to the dynamic interaction—the social media components, active learning tools and real-time results—Coursera and other education dealers are now peddling. Students make up a wide array of knowledge seekers, some are in fact following scholarly passions, others looking for a career change, launch or expand a business, and some simply doing it for fun. But, the clearest indication that a disruptive shift looms for traditional academia is the fact that a Coursera student can now earn the equivalent of a bachelor's degree for which universities like Stanford charge $41,000 per year, online, on their own time, with a more personalized experience, for free. And that poses a problem traditional academia may have to keep trying until they get the right solution. And, unfortunately for them, that is not a class offered by Coursera.

Fast Company Magazine, September 2012, The Coursera Effect. Anya Kamenetz

CLOUD COMPUTING: DISRUPTIVE CLOUDS ON THE HORIZON

A prominent phrase in Clayton Christensen's "The Innovator's Dilemma" is, "Disruptive clouds are on the horizon," which is a very fitting title for this topic. Not to say the cloud is necessarily a new disruption, a novelty for most companies say less than five years ago, has now become a necessity rather than a luxury, and is totally altering the way companies operate at their foundational core.

Thus far, the cloud computing progression has evolved in two primary phases. The first is simply the increased adoption and migration of businesses to the cloud. Internal documents, e-mail and back-end business applications (think customer databases) were the first to get migrated as IT departments became an unnecessary expense. Rather, CIOs realized they could cut maintenance costs by outsourcing the storage of their data, to 3rd party cloud computing service providers. This exodus from traditional data storage to the cloud marks one of the most massive transfers in the history of HR in established companies, and is poised to upend the financial sector. From 2010 to 2020 cloud computing will increase six fold, to $240 billion from $40.7 billion, according to analysts at Forrester research. Despite the tremendous opportunity and extraordinary numbers the first phase of cloud computing represents, early adopters are pushing farther, faster and advancing the sector to where simply being on the cloud has started to become passé. The second, and latest phase of cloud computing has been for companies to figure out how to operate from the cloud. CIOs now see the cloud as an engine of innovation. Companies are asking how they can use the cloud to expand, evolve or pivot their current business models in an effort to create and market new products in order to drive new revenue streams. The long-term, big picture play for companies operating from this vantage point is being able to use cloud efficiencies and agility to drive the top line quicker and beyond. What type of opportunity this second phase represents is unknown, but very exciting.

Gartner Inc. made some predictions as to what's coming in the next four years of cloud computing. Here's their view:

In 2013, the cloud computing market will be worth $150 billion.

In 2014, the personal cloud will replace the personal computer as the center of a user's digital life.

In 2015, prices for 80 percent of cloud services will include a global energy surcharge.

In 2016, 40 percent of enterprises will make proof of independent security testing a precondition for using any type of cloud service.

In 2016, more than 50 percent of the world's 1,000 largest companies will have stored customer-sensitive data in the public cloud.

Clayton Christensen teaches us that disruptive technology attacks so precisely that it becomes the new sustainable technology, until the cycle repeats and the new disruptor dethrones the current champ. And, it seems with all the cloud computing advancements, the disruptive clouds have moved passed the horizon.

WORKDAY'S SWEET REVENGE: BEATING UP LARRY ELLISON AND ORACLE IN THE CLOUD

In 2003, Larry Ellison and Oracle made an offer to purchase a software company called PeopleSoft for $5.1 billion cash—a 6 percent discount. It also announced, assuming the deal went through, that it would fire 5,000 of the company's 12,000 employees. It was typical Larry Ellison in traditional hostile takeover mode. In 2004, after lowballing the purchase price, threatening to shoot the CEO's dog at one point and planning a major employee restructuring, Oracle acquired PeopleSoft for $10.3 billion which sent Dave Duffield (founder and Strategy Manager and eventual Vice Chairman) into early retirement. Duffield is the opposite of Ellison, and built PeopleSoft as a company who took care of its customers and employees. "It was the worst moment of my life," Duffield says, "I had no thought of trying to start over."

And why should he? In his seventies, Duffield should've sat back and enjoyed retirement. He's spent 50 years building high-growth technology companies, and is worth billions. Yet, the higher calling summoned him. Months after PeopleSoft's hostile takeover, he and Bhusri cofounded Workday.

Workday is a major innovator in the cloud computing world. The fast growing high tech startup sells HR and financial software to corporate clients. Workday has 300 plus corporate customers, from Time Warner to Netflix, and in 2011 doubled its sales to more than $300 million while expecting to breach $500 million in 2012 (the year Ashlee Vance wrote about Workday in Bloomberg BusinessWeek, check for updates since). Prominent investors comprised of Reid Hoffman (LinkedIn cofounder), Michael Dell (founder and CEO of Dell) and Jeff Bezos (CEO of Amazon) have backed the company with more than $250 million, which valued the company over $2 billion with clear plans to go public.

Workday's cloud computing model makes mundane tasks, like managing personnel departments, payroll and other back-end assignments, easier and less expensive. This is accomplished by the fact that clients don't have to install and maintain their software in-house. Rather, Workday runs the software in its own data centers and clients simply connect over the Internet, and use the applications. Here is an example Vance gives, about the ease of use of Workday products: While on a business trip in Malaysia, Michael Zill, CIO of medical technology supplier CareFusion, opened the Workday app on his phone, while sitting at a bar after work. A list of to-do tasks appeared on the screen. Zill clicked on an item—a potential hire—and reviewed the notes compiled by his coworkers. Convinced by the notes and the potential hire's experience, Zill hit the approval button and hired the new worker while in a different country, over an app on his smartphone, all while enjoying a beer. Since its origin, business software has a reputation of being difficult to use, inefficient and lacking style (a definite understatement). When Workday launched, Bhusri worked with the engineers to craft the company strategy and made it a point to develop the company's software in a way that makes its use as easy as any other Web 2.0 application, so anyone could use it.

It is a somewhat difficult process to migrate a client's data from their existing system to Workday's servers, but the long-term payout is there, and most companies understand that it is a necessary step, with cloud computing now being industry commonplace. Companies that don't make the move could risk the real threat of becoming obsolete in a climate of efficiency and real-time results, which the cloud also offers. And with that, Workday has been able to pry corporate clients away from competitors like SAP and Oracle.

The biggest risk Workday faces is that competitors like, SAP and Oracle, will wake up and realize Workday is poaching its customers, and take the cloud computing opportunity more seriously which has started happening—June 2012 Oracle released its version of cloud computing software called Oracle Cloud, and has made a number of high-profiled cloud computing service provider acquisitions. But Duffield is not concerned, if anything, he says, "Oracle has validated the cloud and our business model."

Duffield and Bhusri, swear that Workday is not a vendetta based revenge prospect against Ellison. Together, the co-CEOs, own more than half of the company and have a magnificent vision to accomplish, which Duffield credits Larry Ellison for giving them the opportunity. I mean, without the Oracle hostile takeover of PeopleSoft, the insulting low ball offers Oracle pushed for, laying almost half of the PeopleSoft employee workforce off (which has now become the Workday workforce), Ellison being too short-sighted to get into the cloud computing space quickly enough to leave room for new entrants and opportunity for a new, agile, more efficient startup the chance to steal away Oracle's coveted clients—Workday would never have been created.

So, yea, Duffield is right in crediting Larry Ellison with basically paving the way for Workday, knowingly, or not.

Bloomberg BusinessWeek, Optimize June 2012, The Two Horsemen of the Enterprise Software Apocalypse. Ashlee Vance

Newsbeast, February 2012, Cash Cloud, Dan Lyons

BAXTER:
LEADING THE ROBOT REVOLUTION

Meet Baxter, the humanoid robot that moves more like a human than machine—Baxter doesn't and wasn't designed to move in the sharp, precise way typically associated with robots. Baxter, that looks more like a human than machine—Baxter has two arms, a torso, a head and two eyes that communicate human-like expressions (focused, surprised, confused and sad). Baxter that even thinks more like a human than machine—Baxter is trained the way humans learn, by having someone show him how to do something rather than be programmed by experts.

Rethink Robotics is the top-secret startup founded by renowned AI scientist Rodney Brooks—Brooks, perhaps the most praised Artificial Intelligence engineer on the planet—and father of Baxter. Brooks' mission was to cure an issue that has plagued the AI community since its creation: how to construct robots with human abilities. Not only has Brooks executed this, with Baxter, he has accomplished so much more. Baxter is ridiculously easy to use, capable of handling a myriad of tasks, and is insultingly cheap. Brooks' vision for Baxter is so grand it's borderline insane: to replace humans in millions of jobs in the US alone (which Brooks argues is a good thing because workers will get better jobs) and revolutionize the way work gets done in order to enhance the economics of labor.

Prior to launching Rethink Robotics, Rodney Brooks led a successful career as head of MIT's Computer Science and Artificial Intelligence Lab. He stepped down from the prominent position in 2007, to get back in the trenches of hands-on robotics he enjoyed in his early career. Back in the 80's, Brooks became the clear leader in AI by building machines that had real-world application and were inexpensive. His main mission at that time was to create robots that could integrate into everyday life. This goal led to the creation of iRobot, a startup he cofounded in 1990, which won him accolades with the company's winning product, the Roomba. The Roomba is a hugely successful vacuuming robot, and became the first commercialized mass-robot-product for the home. iRobot made more than a million robots in 2011 and the company's top-line revenue tops $465 million.

Home appliances proved an unforeseen sweet spot in the mass-robotics market, and Brooks became obsessed in finding another niche. He researched different markets and industries looking for inefficiencies and opportunities. He finally came across the manufacturing sector and dissected labor statistics, which helped him pinpoint materials handling. Materials handling is essentially picking up items and putting them down, normally on an assembly line. As Brooks explains, "I wanted to take robotics to the next stage by bringing out a game-changing robot for manufacturing companies. One that, compared with existing industrial robots, would be easier to deploy, more useful, and much, much cheaper—making it affordable even to small companies."

What he found when analyzing the manufacturing niche was that he could build a robot that could handle a large list of jobs based on difficulty of task. More specifically, it was a list of jobs performed by 800,000 humans in the U.S. and that is just the start. In 2013, Baxter is projected to replace the 800,000 jobs, 2018 could potentially supplant 11 million and by 2023 has he promise to make 30 million human positions disappear.

A number of reasons contribute to Baxter potentially being the go-to bot. First of all, cost. Industrial robots have long been handling heavy-duty tasks like spray painting and welding for large automotive corporations but run $100,000 or more, plus $200,000 or more to program and set up. Baxter on the other hand costs $22,000 all in, which can easily pay for itself in months, saving a company $30,000 a year or more in labor costs per robot. From the genesis, Brooks forced his team to focus on low-cost solutions and outsources all manufacturing, which result in Baxter being profitable at a low volume and accessible to a wider range of companies.

Next, is the safety factor, which Brooks was as relentless as he was about cost. Industrial robots have to be operated in caged areas away from workers to avoid the risk of serious injury or even death to its human coworkers. Baxter has a slew of safety features such as cameras and sonar sensors that monitor the surrounding area, so it "knows" when someone is near and freezes when there's risk of impact. Baxter has facial expressions on its face-like home screen that serve as warnings; natural expression means he is ready to train, asleep means he is on standby, concentrating is learning a task, focused means working away without a problem, confused means he is having trouble completing a task, sad means he has given up on a task and surprised means a human has approached and, worst case, if someone shows a body part too quickly for Baxter to react, the pressure of the impact on the robot's plastic flesh skin triggers an instant halt to all motion with the result being that Baxter can't deliver anything more than a soft tap.

The most impressive factor of Baxter's design is the way he warns as compared to industrial bots which are carefully set up and programmed by experts to perform actions to precisions of one-hundredth of an inch, repeatedly, without any deviation. Unlike his archaic ancestor, Baxter is trained the way humans warn by having someone show him how to complete the task. Baxter can be trained by anyone, simply by guiding one or both of its arms over the widget it is tasked to pick up, and to the box it is to place the widget in, or whatever the task may be, following easy to understand menu prompts. These elements of Baxter's design are not by coincidence, but are calculated procedures Brooks derived from his success of the Roomba. The laws work to guide him and his team during development, and are rules such as robots should not be humanoid just for the sake of making them look like humans, and get something out that's so laden with breakthrough capabilities at such a low price that the competition will be crushed before it exists.

Although Brooks' commandments have served him exceedingly well thus far, Brooks and Rethink Robots have their work cut out for them. For starters, Baxter must work as expected, with little to no error, on a massive scale. Rethink will have to forcefully persuade small to mid-size manufacturing plants that they are ready for robots. On top of all that, quite possibly their highlight hurdle—in a time when jobs, jobs, jobs is a main topic of politics and economics—is the resistance companies may have outsourcing human jobs to robots. And yet, in spite of a seemingly uphill battle, the robot revolution is here. And Baxter's future is very bright, not just because Amazon founder and warehouse-automation forerunner Jeff Bezos was Rethink's first investor, nor the fact that Rethink plans to encourage programmers to take Baxter in different directions with its open source platform—but because Baxter's maker programmed him for greatness.

Inc. Magazine, October 2012, The Rise of the Robotic Workforce. David Friedman

CARL BASS AND AUTODESK: STARING DOWN THE INNOVATOR'S DILEMMA

Carl Bass, 55 (at the time of this writing); is CEO and President of Autodesk—one of the world's leading makers of sophisticated 3-D design software for engineers, architects and artists worth $7 billion on the capital markets, and Maker Movement die hard— he is an amateur woodworker. With Carl Bass at its helm, Autodesk has interestingly positioned itself and adjusted its long-term strategy to take advantage of makers and garage entrepreneurs—who make up the DIY Maker Movement. "Some people see it as a niche market. They claim it can't be possibly scale. But this is a trend, not a fad—something seismic is going on," says Bass.

Under Bass' direction, Autodesk has put its money where its CEOs long-term vision is— the corporation has launched new products in its consumer-focused 123D line, developing an array of low-cost modeling apps for PCs and tablets. In the same moment, they are enjoying a shopping high—after purchasing Instructables (a design sharing community), Pixlr (a photo-editing site) and Socialcam (an app for video editing and sharing on mobile devices).

As Bob Parks of Wired says, on paper, no firm is better to take advantage of a maker-led future than Autodesk, whose 30 years of experience in computer-aided design give it unparalleled intelligence about the capabilities that designers want and need in their software. Interesting theory, but "on paper" rarely translates to real world—if that was the case, every company in history that ever disrupted an industry would've never had a shot. Plus, do the past 30 years have unparalleled relevancy to today's cloud computing, mobile dominant powered real time focused environment? I don't know but, Autodesk will face challenges, and already has. For starters, 123D—Autodesk's freeware modeling app—received negative reviews with focus groups and is being upgraded. It will have to simplify its already powerful software tools, that can cost anywhere from $1,000 to upwards of $50,000 per user, into user-friendly apps at a low cost or even Freemium business model. Most challenging however, is the simple fact that Autodesk will have to persuade the grass-roots, hobbyist Maker Movement, accustomed to interacting with amateurs like themselves, that a multibillion-dollar corporation has an authentic and transparent agenda with the community's best interest at heart.

Autodesk's raid into the maker community is not on a whim. In 2009, a product manager built an iPhone mobile app version of Sketchbook Pro—a professional software tool for artists and industrial designers—and priced it around one hundred bucks. Bass initially balked at the idea, until two months and roughly a million downloads later—making it the fastest-moving software program in Autodesk's history—he had a change of heart. By 2010, the app was released on the iPad and the Android operating platform. To put it in perspective, in its 30-year history, Autodesk had sold only 12 million copies of the desktop version of Sketchbook Pro, and by October 2012, only three years after its release, 10 million consumers had downloaded the app version of Sketchbook Pro. It became blatantly obvious that there was a clear demand for consumer based Autodesk products and by May 2011, the company had released 123D—their free 3-D modeling software. From that point, Autodesk blitzed the line and released a myriad of products running on the Freemium model—123D Catch, which allows users to manipulate colors and textures to make 3-D art and 123D Make that helps users to construct real-life versions of their own onscreen creations by stacking or building with flat materials like cardboard or sheet metal.

Autodesk's latest professional software (as of October 2012) actually aids in the design. As Autodesk's Kowalski explains, for example, the software can analyze architectural designs for energy efficiency or tell you how a building would respond to an earthquake. It examines aircraft parts for structural strength and shows engineers where the pieces are most likely to break. The plan is that Autodesk's consumer apps will harness this same predictive algorithm technology to assist in design as well. Through these consumer apps and professional GRAPE software, simplified for anyone to use, Autodesk attempts to cross the early adopter maker market chasm into the mainstream.

Autodesk seems to be making the right moves in order to make the transition into the DIY community. Through recent acquisitions, Autodesk has extended its reach—the Pixlr and Instructables purchases empowered Autodesk with roughly 35 million monthly unique web visitors, catapulting it ahead of Pinterest (around 23 million) and Tumblr (27 million): include Socialcam's 16 million users and Autodesk's total online reach is comparable to Twitter and LinkedIn (source: Wired, October 2012). Add to that, Autodesk's recent investment in TechShop—a chain of workshops where DIY'ers collaborate, share access to high-end software and hardware tools, to model and build their various inventions—and it appears Autodesk is doing everything right; listening to customers, making community focused acquisitions and filling in the voids left in the industry and yet, is this not the absolute dilemma Christensen poses in the classic, The Innovator's Dilemma. The thesis question the book attempts to answer is why do great companies fail? Clayton Christensen states this, "That's why we call it the innovator's dilemma: doing the right thing is the wrong thing."

Put me in Carl Bass' shoes and I take Christensen's teachings to heart: maybe I spin out a couple stand-alone entities to pursue certain avenues that show promise in the maker community, I harness the power of the cloud to improve customers' computing efficiency and force, I test rigorously with minimum viable products, rather than creating totally new products, I construct a novel product architecture with proven products and keep them basic and easy to use, rather than defend my company's position in the marketplace, I let the market demand prove my value and I fail quickly to learn as fast as possible—maybe even under different D.B.A.s as to not tarnish the Autodesk reputation. Carl Bass is facing a real dilemma, and he even admits he hasn't quite figured out how Autodesk will make money from all these consumer ventures. But one thing is certain, he is right in saying something 'seismic is going on,' I just hope for Carl's sake it is not the crumbling of a $7 billion publicly traded software company's footing, through the shift towards a more decentralized grass-roots movement, disrupting all established firms that stand in its way.

Wired Magazine, September 2012, Creation Engine: Autodesk Wants to Help Anyone, Anywhere, Make Anything. Bob Parks

FUNDING STRATEGY: UNDERSTANDING THE LAWS OF ACCESSING FRESH CAPITAL VIA CROWDFUNDING

In an astounding and almost unheard of act of bipartnership, in April 2012, Congress passed the JOBS Act. The JOBS Act is a new law that allows startups to find investors online via crowdfunding.

Essentially, the JOBS Act creates an entirely new avenue for startups to sell equity and potentially raise a ton of money for their company—through crowdfunding. Crowdfunding itself is not a new technique—being that entrepreneurs can use the masses (the crowd) to raise small amounts of capital from many investors (the funding). However, the money raised currently (November 2012), is classified as a donation rather than investment, and donors receive perks from the companies like the ability to preorder products. Notable crowdfunding sites like Kickstarter and Indiegogo contributed to the roughly $1.5 billion total crowdfunding platforms raised alone in 2011.

There is an issue however, even though Congress passed the law, the Securities and Exchange Commission has stalled in implementing the law. The reason most likely the SEC is dragging its heels is because the law will do away with some regulations—of course those that prevent startups from offering shares of their company through crowdfunding. For instance, the SEC has long banned private companies from publicly soliciting investors, including through the internet. Also, there are SEC rules that limit how many investors a private company may have before it is forced to register with the SEC. Another benefit for startups through the JOBS Act is who they will be able to tap for funding. Currently, entrepreneurs must limit their pitches to wealthy, accredited investors, but through the Act, investors making less than $100,000 per year will be able to invest up to 5 percent of their income in startups, and those making $150,000 or more will be permitted to invest up to 10 percent of their annual income. The question still remains, however, whether or not the SEC will require crowdfunding sites to verify the income of investors. Ironing out these types of details is most likely hindering the SEC from implementing the Act, but the SEC should be able to finalize everything by latest start of 2013.

The crowdfunding demand is apparent and the industry grew 63 percent in 2011 alone, with hundreds of new crowdfunding sites gearing up to launch (Inc. Magazine, November 2012). And sites like Crowd Control are springing up which help entrepreneurs navigate new crowdfunding laws by acting as a 'disclosure and due diligence advisor.'

Even with the obstacles, at least the government and SEC recognize the importance of easing regulations for startups seeking funding. Fundraising by far is the most difficult part of launching a startup, the least government can do is open up some new avenues to accessing capital.

Inc. Magazine, November 2012, Crowd Control, Crowdfunding Startups Hit Speed Bumps. Ryan Underwood

Entrepreneur Magazine, November 2012, CrowdCheck Helps Startups Navigate Crowdfunding Laws. Michelle Goodman

PROTEUS' SMART PILL: THE PILL WITH INTELLIGENCE

What if the pill you just swallowed could monitor dosages, track your heart rate and other bodily functions, and send the information to your smartphone? Thanks to Proteus Digital Health, a private Northern CA company whose attracted upwards of $125 million in private funding, that soon may be a reality.

As John Mcdermott of Inc. Magazine, reported in November 2012, Proteus has created a "smart pill" system, with a pill that contains a sensor which communicates with a patch on the torso once the pill mixes with stomach fluid. The patch communicates information about the type of pill, when it was digested, heart rate, respiration and activity level of the patient, to a nearby smartphone where the information can be accessed on a mobile app. This system enables that patients will take the right amount of medication, at the right time and focus initially on people with diabetes and central nervous system disorders, although the uses are endless.

Inc. Magazine, November 2012, Innovation: Companies on the Cutting Edge. John McDermott

INVESTMENT STRATEGY: WHAT VCS REALLY WANT

What if you knew what VC's were thinking? In November 2012, Daniel Stolle published an article in Inc. Magazine showcasing a study conducted by Rolf Wüstenhagen and Nina Hampl of the University of St. Gallen in Switzerland and Robert Wuebker of the University of Utah, that showed what variables mattered most to VCs when deciding to invest, to get inside the mind of VCs.

The researchers used conjoint analysis, which asks indirect questions that get respondents to reveal how they will prioritize different variables. The researchers sent out an e-mail survey to 86 venture capitalists that gave a series of scenarios involving hypothetical early-stage clean energy company seeking its first professional round of funding. Researchers manipulated factors like product development—something VCs were told the product was still in inception stage, other times that the product was completed and ready to launch—and the founders' backgrounds—sometimes VCs were told founders were fresh out of grad school, while other times that they had run previous startups. Not surprisingly, the potential return of an investment held the most weight, at 30.4 percent, in helping a VC decide to invest or not. Founders' experience (27%) and the product's market readings (26.4%) also weighed in heavily. Regulatory exposure made up 6.6 percent, 6.4 percent that VCs had a social connection with founders and 3.2 percent accounted for the identity of the lead investor (say another prominent VC firm or angel investor).

The takeaway: the old adage, 'We invest in the jockey, not the horse' did not necessarily play out in the researchers' findings seeing as how potential return outweighed founders' experience. Another notable find was the fact that having a social connection to the founders was more important than the identity of the lead investor. The bottom-line is although a social connection may help you get a foot in the door, the business potential outweighs everything. Keep this in mind when creating investment documentation and pitching investors.

Inc. Magazine, November 2012, How VCs Think. Daniel Stolle

MEET WATSON: IBM'S SUPERCOMPUTER THAT SPEAKS AND UNDERSTANDS OUR LANGUAGE

Artificial Intelligence is no longer science fiction—Google cars now drive themselves, Apple's Siri talks to you and IBM's supercomputer named Watson gets its information not by hand-coded programming, but by reading. Yes, Watson gained all of its knowledge by simply reading all of Wikipedia.

'Simply reading' may be the understatement of the century, it's necessary to understand the significance. Rather than communicate in 1s and 0s—machine language, Watson understands natural language—human language. That is its sole reason for existence—to be able to comprehend the complexities of human language. To show its brilliance, the Watson IBM Skunk Works computer engineering team had one simple objective: to beat the Jeopardy champions at their own game. In February 2011, Watson took the cake.

What does that mean? Look at what Jon Gertner reports after writing an article about Watson, in the November 2012 Fast Company issue: Our past year, IBM executives have come to believe that Watson represents the first machine of The Third Computer Age, a category now referred to within the company as cognitive computing. As John Kelly, IBM's Chief of Research, describes it to Gertner, "The first generation of computers were tabulating machines that added up figures, the second generation were the programmable systems—the mainframe, the first IBM 360, PCs, all the computers we have today. Now, we've arrived at the cognitive moment—a moment of true artificial intelligence. These computers, such as Watson can recognize important content within language, both written and spoken. They do not ask us to communicate with them in their coded language; they speak ours. And perhaps most important, they can learn, so they improve without constant human instruction."

Although, like other computers, Watson crawls the web and scours vast databases when answering an inquiry—the process in which Watson deciphers the information is totally unique to all other computers. Watson translates the information in human terms, and as David

Ferrucci, the IBM researcher who led the team that built the first Watson says, "its saying: 'What does this mean to me?' And that's a big deal."

In mere seconds when solving a problem, Watson amasses hundreds of thousands of answers from a boundless data base, next, Watson corrals all of the solutions, then sifts through them with its set of algorithms and produces a series of the richest solutions; each substantiated with Watson's evidence all ranked by levels of probability, in their viability. As computer science explains, this makes Watson probabilistic more correctly than deterministic. And much to Hollywood's dismay of an apocalyptic Skynet-depiction of the robot doomsday, Watson is here to help us—not supersede us, to add support to our questions not actually solve them.

Watson differs from mainframes in another even more practical and remarkable way. The most powerful modern age computers excel at managing large amounts of structured information, which is clearly defined data comprised of stats, facts and numbers. However, thanks in part to the open source nature of the Internet, the proliferation of social media and user generated content like blogs, user reviews and e-mails, the ease and high frequency of computing via mobile technology, and information created by our machines, sensors, and apps, the world's data is much more undefined, obscure and lies outside the scope of modern computing power. This is the subsequent reason for the rapid increase of startups, with the sole mission to organize and bring quality to the world's "Big Data." Part of Watson's brilliance, on the other hand, is its ability to understand and comprehend unstructured information. On this big data front, the implications for Watson are endless.

At the time of this writing (November 2012), Gertner writes that there are only half-a-dozen Watsons scattered across the country, with some on site and others which are cloud based. "That's the reality of it," Bernie Meyerson, IBM's VP of innovation tells Gertner, "Effectively, there's no limit to how many Watsons there can be. Watson is a creation of software, not hardware."

So what's next for Watson? The actual business model for Watson is still unclear, and IBM hasn't decided whether to sell Watson as hardware (a computer) or as software (the service). One of Watson's current goals is to prove its credibility and substantiate its value, with IBM's current clients. Another goal, as the IBM team creates the next iteration— Watson 2.0—is for Watson to become more practical and cut down its time to prepare for a new discipline—say finance or medicine. John Kelly believes that eventually Watson will shrink to the size of a handheld device. But to predict how soon Watson will spread among the general public masses would've been like forecasting the permeation of the PC—near impossible. Although IBM claims that Watson will begin to scale dramatically late next year (2013), and says they have built the technology, demonstrated it, built the tooling and methods around it; they have the recipe book and plan to just 'push it out.' Like proud parents, Watson's creators are excited to see what it can accomplish out on its own, its public raid seems inevitable and is positioned to change the course of history—and lucky for our sake, Watson seems to be coming as friend not foe.

Fast Company, November 2012, Calling Dr. Watson. Jon Gertner

AARON LEVIE OF BOX THE PARANOID DISRUPTOR IN THE CLOUDS

Aaron Levie is like the Mark Zuckerberg of cloud storage—he is nerdy, in his late twenties and runs a billion-plus dollar valued company. Levie started building websites at age 13, and by 20 cofounded Box.Net—which gives businesses a secure way to share content online and on mobile devices. Since its founding, the company has attracted upwards of $100 million in venture funding from prominent VCs including Andreesen & Horowitz, employs 600-plus people, has more than doubled sales every year, and stores several thousand terabytes of information for more than 100,000 clients.

Levie says his main goals are to innovate and to disrupt, "I want to disrupt the marketplace and to disrupt the old model—the way traditional software companies have created and sold their storage products and interacted with customers. Also, I want to avoid being disrupted. Our big goals for this year were to more than double our sales, to go international, and to shift from only direct sales to also working with partners to sell our products." And although his "disrupting goals" sounds super cliché, he says Box was on track to meet his business goals and overachieve on sales growth.

Like Jobs before him, Dorsey, and Zuckerberg, Levie is hands-on with his product design and engineering team. Nobody in the company has a private office, in order to foster collaboration and Levie claims he is addicted to speed and efficiency because Box is competing against companies that have tens of thousands of people.

Levie built the Box Foundation on a set of key core values. One such value, which he states, is the biggest value he provides to the company's culture, is to constantly punch on the scale of opportunity—to help the company realize they can do something 10 times bigger, 10 times faster, 10 times better. Another core value is to simply "get shit done," which Levie says contributes to a very execution-oriented culture, the opposite of a bureaucratic slow decision making culture. Additionally, and perhaps my favorite of Box's values is "make mom proud (unless she's evil)." Lastly, adopted from that social media giant with the blue and white logo is to "take risk, fail fast," which he explains that if the company fails fast, they can correct mistakes quickly.

106

Levie is relentless in the hours he keeps, and around 8pm every night at the office he takes a nap for 18-25 minutes (he's experimenting with the optimal rest time) and starts his second day. He spends his second day analyzing news headlines and the competitive landscape, reads business books including a couple of his favorites—The Innovator's Dilemma, Crossing the Chasm and Blue Ocean Strategy (all timeless classics) and gathers different data points to forecast the company's future strategy. He says, "The companies that win are the companies that guess the future right and take their vision to the world." So far Levie has guessed right, but his paranoia about being disrupted is justified—he never knows what hotshot up-and-coming tech visionary is taking aim at the target he has become, and the more his company grows, the larger and larger the target he becomes.

Inc. Magazine, November 2012, The Way I Work. Reshma Memon Yaqub

LEGAL STRATEGY: UNDERSTANDING DESIGN DEFENSE

Design patents have become a hot topic in the tech world and a powerful weapon in the tech battle for dominance. Cooper Woodring, an industrial designer and the former Industrial Designers Society of America's President, was instrumental in helping secure Apple's victory over Samsung, in possibly the most notable design suit to date. $1.05 billion dollars later, Apple and the rest of the tech world are taking heed to the power of the patent. November 2012, Fast Company interviewed Woodring to better understand the intricacies and tricks in how to best utilize a design patent.

A utility patent protects the way a product functions, is the most common patent and has historically been the main character in litigation. However, as opposed to twenty years ago when design patents provided too many precise details in their filings, today's companies only patent the main parts, which has led to a rise in use and value of the design patent. Previously, as Woodring explains, if a filer provides all of the complex details in its sketches, then copycats could argue that their product was different if they changed the minutest of details. "Now companies only patent the parts of a product that represents its 'heart and soul' like Apple's 'flat, transparent, edge-to-edge front and rounded corners.' That's new and enforceable," Woodring asserts.

In determining if a product is too similar to a competitor's or the rest of the industry, the standing criterion is enforced by "the eye of an ordinary observer." As Woodring accounts, "The law dates back to 1871, when the court determined then that it wasn't professional buyers who should decide an infringement case but rather common consumers. If rulings were based on the opinions of experts, who could never be received, design patents would be worthless."

Woodring has been so dynamic and successful in his brandishing of design patents that the "Woodring strategy" has been coined. Woodring says that the strategy is deployed when a company releases a product that looks similar to the patented design of another company's product. It involves designing a third version that doesn't look anything like the other two, proving there's more than one design that could fulfill a product's function. The oddball design, makes the other two look like kissing cousins by comparison.

With the recent increase in the use of design patents, and Apple's billion dollar win, the concern has become that design patents will suffocate innovation. But Woodring disagrees, and believes the opposite is true, that design patents will cause others to create entirely new products, which is a good thing for design. And I can't help but agree.

Fast Company, November 2012, Dean of the Design Defense. Linda Tischler

GOOGLE: THE [COMPUTING] FORCE IS STRONG IN THIS ONE

The big five tech titans—Facebook, Apple, Microsoft, Amazon and Google—are in a no hold bar, multi-platformed battle to the death. The victor's spoils? Control of our digital lives. For instance, the tablet front runner Apple is being flanked from Amazon, Google and Microsoft over the market. The smartphone industry is an arms race between Microsoft, Apple and Google. While war in the social network space is being waged amongst Facebook, Microsoft and Google Video (TV, movies), music and cloud services are under attack by every party except Facebook. Even Google's flagship product Search is being infiltrated by Microsoft, and Facebook is rumored to join the fight. If you look closely, however, there is one common denominator in every battle—a single foe. As all encompassing, swift and quiet as dark, heavy rain clouds taking over the clear, blue sky, Google has established major positions in each battlefield front.

And although each of the aforementioned applications are consumer facing, Google's might and force is derived from a source the public never sees, and rarely hears about. As Steven Levy of Wired puts it, "What makes Google Google is its physical network, its thousands of fiber miles, and those many thousands of servers that, in aggregate, add up to the mother of all clouds. This multi-billion dollar infrastructure allows the company to index 20 billion web pages a day. To handle more than 3 billion daily search queries. To conduct millions of ad auctions in real time. To offer free e-mail storage to 425 million Gmail users. To zip millions of YouTube videos to users every day. To deliver search results before the user has finished typing the query. In the near future, when Google releases the wearable computing platform called "Glass," this infrastructure will power its visual search results. Crucial to Google's success has been its ability to build, organize and operate [this] huge network of servers and fiber-optic cables with an efficiency and speed that rocks physics on its heels. Google has spread its infrastructure across a global archipelago of massive buildings—a dozen or so information palaces in locales as diverse as Council Bluffs, Iowa; St. Ghislain, Belgium; and soon Hong Kong and Singapore—where an unspecified but huge number of machines process and deliver the continuing chronicle of human experience.

For years, Google kept a tight confidential policy about its engineering prowess. The reason being that its army of servers and computer network empire was its core advantage, and revealing secrets would be like an attacking army giving its enemy the strategy in which it plans to implement in the heart of battle. That was, until recently. But before we unveil what changed, let's rewind time and take it back to Google's more humbling beginnings.

Google did not start out in life with the extravagant network regime they now boast of. In fact, in February of 1999, Google's server facility was living like a college student living in a dorm room—sharing space at a colocation site, a server facility where a multitude of companies rent floor space and server capabilities. The issue though—Google was maturing, and as we learn through Steven Levy, Google was not only processing millions of queries every week, but increasing the frequency in which it indexed the web—gathering every bit of online information and putting it into a searchable format. AdWords—the service that invited advertisers to bid for placement alongside search results relevant to their wares—involved computation-heavy processes that were just as demanding as Search. New applications were being developed, and on top of it all, was the fact that the tech downturn that plagued the 90's looked to be coming to an end—meaning, Google's future leasing deals would become much more expensive. The current system took 3.5 seconds to deliver search results, crashed on Mondays and would not suffice in supporting Google's rapid growth.

Google determined in order for it to prosper, it would have to strike out on its own—to build and operate its own data centers, and determine how to do it less costly and more efficiently than anyone in the industry. A dedicated team set out to accomplish the mission, and codenamed the secret operation—Willpower. The special ops team worked efficiently and unearthed a number of epiphanies—such as, the fact that server rooms did not need to be kept so cold, innovative ways to cool server room water, uncovered sources of waste and upgraded those processes—which led to unheard-of energy savings, which significantly dropped the cost of operating its data centers.

The victory however, was bittersweet: first, the energy efficiency and cost-saving allowed its data centers to thrive, which facilitated Google's explosive growth and ultimately contributed to Google's supreme dominance. Keeping its practices undercover afforded it an unprecedented competitive advantage but, the flip to that was if the industry saw how much energy Google was saving, an effort would be made to beat Google's results, which could lead to a widely positive environmental impact (seeing as now data centers consume up to 1.5 percent of worldwide electricity use). So Google stuck to its company-wide mission, "don't be evil," and in 2009 announced its most recent power usage effectiveness results (PUE— the standard measure of data center efficiency), and hinted at some of its techniques. The announcement marked a revolution for the industry. Thanks to Google, a new benchmark has been set in terms of data power efficiency, and companies like Facebook and Yahoo now report similar PUEs.

Understanding the power, importance and vastness of Google's server network, one can't help but beget the question of how many servers does Google put to use? Which is a question Google has danced around for years now (since building its first data center), simply maintaining the position of "hundreds of thousands." In 2012, however, Steven Levy was blessed with a rare backstage VIP access to one of Google's data centers in Lenoir, North Carolina. He states in the Lenoir facility alone, at the time of his visit, 49,923 servers were operating. In addition, he explains that later when visiting Google's data center R&D facility in Mountain View, CA, he came across a small plaque that read 'July 9, 2008. Google's Millionth Server.' He says that executives commented that the number was cumulative though, and not necessarily an indication that Google has a million servers running at once. And with that, Levy realized that the magic number, if even obtainable, is basically meaningless. That today's machines, with multicore processors and other advances, have many times the power and utility of earlier versions. A single Google server circa 2012 may be the equivalent of 20 servers from a previous generation. And in any case Google thinks in terms of clusters—huge numbers of machines that act together to provide a service or run an application—which yields computer power as an abstract metric, not merely by individual servers. Besides, Google's seemingly so far advanced in terms of its competitors, that its past technology is merely today's standard, and its today's system will be tomorrow's. So in order to understand its today's operations, we'll have to sit back and wait for tomorrow.

Wired Magazine, November 2012, The Warships of Silicon Valley. Joe Kloc
Wired Magazine, November 2012, Deep Inside a Google Data Center. Steven Levy

ELON MUSK: THE REAL IRON MAN

I have a hero—his name is Elon Musk, and I'm not the only one who looks up to him. In fact, an entire superhero franchise is based on him. As Ashlee Vance explains, Jon Favreau, a friend and the director of the Iron Man movies, has called Musk the basis for his version of comic book hero Tony Stark, the playboy inventor who builds a flying weaponized suit. Friends and colleagues portray him as Howard Hughes, John D. Rockefeller and Steve Jobs merged into one. As Vance reports, Bruce Leak, a veteran Silicon Valley entrepreneur who worked with Musk previously, says, "He has that Bill Gates energy where his foot bounces and he's wiggling just because he's so smart."

Chris Anderson of Wired says, "Extreme entrepreneurs have an extraordinary ability to believe in their own visions, so much so that they think what they're embarking on isn't really that risky." He claims that he's never met an entrepreneur who fits the mold more than Elon Musk. Of all the entrepreneurs he admires most—Musk, Jeff Bezos, Reed Hastings, Jack Dorsey, Sergey Bin and Larry Page, Bill Gates, Steve Jobs, and a few others—have sought not just to build great companies but to take on problems that really matter. He states, yet even in this class of Universe-denters, Musk stands out.

Musk grew up in Pretoria, South Africa. His parents divorced when he was 9 years old. His dad was an electromechanical engineer, which meant there were lots of "engineer things" around him. And when young Musk asked for an explanation about how something worked, he got the true explanation. Musk and his younger brother Kimbal, enjoyed a great deal of independence while growing up, and both enjoyed creating homemade explosives and building rockets. Musk led his brother and cousins on a myriad of ventures during their childhood, including selling Easter eggs in their neighborhood and started a video game arcade.

By age 15, Musk was ready to take on the world and bought a Canadian passport (where his mother was born and he still had distant family). He spent the year showing up to the houses of distant Canadian relatives, while working odd-end jobs, before making it to Queen's University in Ontario. He spent two years there and then went on to the University of Pennsylvania, where he earned degrees in Physics and Economics. He put himself through Penn by throwing huge parties with his roommate, Adeo Ressi.

In 1995, after spending 2 days in a Stanford graduate program on Applied Physics, he dropped out to start an online publishing platform for the media industry called Zip2, with Kimbal.

By 1999, 4 years later, they sold Zip2 for $307 million to Compaq.

In 2000, he formed PayPal by merging his latest startup X.Com—which was basically an online bank—with Max Levchin and Peter Thiel's Confinity. Musk was the largest shareholder, and for a stint of time its CEO.

2002 marked the year PayPal went public and its stock rose more than 54 percent on its first day of trading. 8 months later, eBay acquired the company for $1.5 billion rewarding Musk $180 million payout.

Musk then parlayed his winnings into a number of new ventures. In 2002, he created Space Exploration Technologies, better known as SpaceX, which is a private space company poised to replace the space shuttle and catapult us into an interplanetary age.

In 2004, he invested into Tesla Motors, a company that manufactures high-performance electric cars.

He funded Everdream, a data-center software company. And 2006, helped build SolarCity which provides solar-power systems to some 33,000 buildings and is expected to go public imminently at a value worth of $1.5 billion.

In 2008, however, Musk's favor took a turn for the worse. His marriage to his college sweetheart collapsed, and was forced to sell his McLaren F1—the most expensive car in the world at that time—during divorce settlements. Tesla was almost forced to shut its doors when it struggled to raise venture funds, due to cost overruns and incessant delays that tarnished Musk's credibility. He sunk his last $3 million into Tesla and had to borrow money from friends. Referring to it all, Musk says, "I was just getting pistol whipped. I was like, 'I'm f*cked. What am I going to do?'"

Then 2009 happened, and Everdream—which Musk was majority shareholder of—was acquired by Dell for $120 million. "That money arrived in early 2009 and replenished the coffers. Thank goodness, man," he reflects.

Musk is CEO of SpaceX and Tesla, and Company Chair of SolarCity. He is majority shareholder of all three companies, and once SolarCity goes public could have a net worth of more than $3 billion.

As Vance writes, if they survive, each company will continue to be improbable and inspiring businesses. In 2012, Musk said the next six months will be about proving things for Tesla. At the time, it produced six Model S's a day, but expects to produce as many as 100 cars per day by the end of the year. Musk inspects every model before it's shipped. The model S begins at roughly $50,000 with federal credits, can seat seven, accelerate from zero to 60 in an astonishing 4.4 seconds, get 300 miles per charge and is establishing unrivaled benchmarks in the electric vehicle space. "We have thousands of reservations for the Model S, and that's without test drives," states George Blankenship, head of Tesla's Retail Division. "This is the first place I've worked that's going to change the world," he says.

SpaceX has already become profitable and is simply working through its backlog of orders. Next year, (2013), SpaceX looks to launch eight flights, and as many as 16 the following year. If it accomplishes those plans it would in fact be carrying out the bulk of the world's commercial spaceflights. In just three years, SpaceX plans to send people to space for $20 million a head versus the $63 million it costs today. SpaceX has been able to build safe, cost-efficient spacecraft, giving it a huge competitive advantage in the private commercial spacecraft industry.

Musk is only getting started—and has even larger visions for the future. He says that he plans to make humanity a multi-planetary species by launching SpaceX spacecraft to Mars in the next 10 to 15 years. He has an idea he dubbed the "hyperloop" which is a tube that can zip people from San Francisco to Los Angeles in 30 minutes, and has plans for a jet that can takeoff vertically. These ideas may sound like total madness, but that's just it. As Chris Anderson says, that's the thing about extreme entrepreneurism: there's a fine line between madness and genius, and you need a little bit of both to really change the world. And change the world is exactly what Musk plans to do.

Wired Magazine, November 2012, Elon Musk's Mission to Mars. Chris Anderson
Bloomberg BusinessWeek, September 2012, Elon Musk, Man of Tomorrow. Ashlee Vance

TED: DISRUPTING ITS OWN BUSINESS

TED (Technology, Entertainment, Design) can easily be called the epicenter of world-changing ideas. For years TED Talks have been an elite, members-only, annual gala, for wealthy Silicon Valley and Hollywood types, hosted in Long Beach, CA. Speakers captivate the audience with earth-shattering ideas, experiments, businesses and outcomes—everything technology, entertainment and design focused (which actually encompasses quite a bit). The thing about TED Talks, however, is that the event itself always seemed so allusive for the mainstream market—with cost being the primary barrier to entry and limited space. Realizing they wanted TED Talks to be more practical and less pie-in-the-sky, in 2006, TED Headquarters put its talks online, which helped democratize the "institution" of TED, and made it widely accessible to anyone rather than the select elite. But TED didn't stop there, to engage a wider audience, in a sense, it turned its entire organization inside out—and in 2008, it introduced TEDx, which became a way for local communities to host TED-like conferences on a smaller, intimate, more grass-roots level.

TED's assumption—that operating from a bottom-up approach, rather than top-down, would engage the masses—has paid off in unequivocal ways. TEDx has spread like wildfire around the globe, 1,300 cities (as of December 2012) in 134 countries, hosting more than 800,000 people in total—a tremendous amount more than have ever attended any official TED event.

Bill Wasik of Wired does a great job of breaking down the ins-and-outs of Tedx. He explains, the creators of the satellite conferences aren't volunteers; they're licenses, who are given latitude to put together events on their own terms, including (with permission) the ability to accept sponsorships and to charge admission of up to $100 per ticket for recouping costs. He says, it's impossible to overstate how much this autonomy, the sense of ownership, has shaped the evolution of TEDx. Ground rules for organizers are straight forward: first, they need to apply for a license under a unique name—multiple TEDxes established in one city is permitted. For instance, San Francisco has more than 15 and Manhattan over 30. Once approved, the license (or licenses—many TEDxes are run by small groups) can program the event any way, with a couple of restrictions. One core rule, true of TED too, is that no sponsors can display logos onstage, and no one—sponsor nor speaker—is allowed to sell anything during the discussions. Also, organizers who have been to TED can sell an endless amount of tickets, but everyone else has to limit their attendance to 150 people. Each TEDx is required to show at least two videos from TED.com, but the rest of the presenters are in person and predominantly locals, resulting in a TED-like experience, across each local market.

TED's use of the tipping point to its advantage has created a contagious epidemic through the vehicle of TEDx. What was once one of the nation's most exclusive and coveted private parties, has opened its guest list to the public and quickly become the most popular gathering in the world. I'm just wondering why it took TED—the organization with the most sought-after crowds, forward thinking leaders and renown experts—so long to realize that the "elite" weren't the only ones with big ideas, and that the mass public actually has something to say.

Wired Magazine, December 2012, Planet TEDx. Bill Wasik

APPLE: THE SPIRIT LIVES ON

October 5, 2011, the tech sector wept, the world mourned, and one of the most valuable companies in the world gave tribute to their fallen hero. The day forever marks the passing of a man turned legend, the end of an era, and yet represented an unequaled culminating opportunity for another equally impressive man.

As Josh Tyrangiel of Bloomberg BusinessWeek writes, "Prior to his death on Oct. 5, 2011, Steve Jobs made sure that the elevation of Tim Cook, his longtime Head of Operations and trusted deputy, to Apple Chief Executive Officer, would be drama-free." He goes, 'I never want you to ask what I would have done, just do what's right.' He was very clear," recalls Cook.

With the passing of Jobs, Tim Cook was catapulted into the limelight of possibly the business world's most famous position—running one of the world's most valuable and innovative companies on the globe. Josh Tyrangiel sat down with Cook for an in-depth interview. And inside look into the technology behemoth, while getting Cook's insight on what makes Apple tick.

Tyrangiel starts off the interview by asking, How has Apple changed since Oct. 5, 2011?"

Cook explains, "That the first thing to realize is that all the things that have made Apple so special are the same as they have always been. That doesn't mean that Apple is the same. Apple has changed every day since I have been here. But the DNA of the company, the thing that makes our heart beat, is a maniacal focus on making the best products in the world. Not good products or a lot of products, but the absolute best products in the world. In creating these great products, we focus on enriching people's lives—a higher cause for the product. These are the macro things that drive the company. They haven't changed. They're not changing. I will not witness or permit those changes because that's what makes the company so special."

Cook's background is extensive and his management experience dates back to 1983 where he started as Director of North American Fulfillment at IBM, after obtaining his MBA at Duke University. He went on to become COO of the Reseller Division for Intelligent Electronics, then Vice President of Corporate Materials at Compaq, before eventually being inaugurated into the Apple family in 1998, as the Senior Vice President of Operations. Prior to taking the reigns full-time, Cook had been interim CEO three times during his Apple calling—once in

2004 when Jobs had back surgery, another when Steve took a medical leave for half a year, and then again in 2011. But being permanent CEO, as he says, "This, you know, (pause). This has been different. So I have had to adjust to that."

And, adjust he has—in his first 16 months on the job, Apple released next-generation iPads and iPhones and witnessed its stock price rise 43 percent. Cook's leadership style is a huge contributing factor and he explains that he is not driven by being recognized, but rather by doing great work, seeing people do incredible things and having a part in that."

In every story that mentions Cook, he is described as a Southern gentleman, an Auburn football fan, early to work and last to leave. He humbly explains that one of his favorite parts of his position are the thousands of daily e-mails he receives from passionate Apple enthusiasts, casually explaining the things they like or thoughts about what could improve. He says, "I love it. I don't know if there's another company on earth this happens with. These are people from all over the world. I look at it, and I go, 'this is a privilege.'"

Cook recalls that during his first day working for Apple, he had to cross a picket line to get into the building. These were customers protesting, because Jobs had discontinued the Newton Device, and they cared so deeply about the product that they showed up to protest.

Part of Apple's magic is that the company has been able to integrate—arguably, better then anyone—hardware, software and services seamlessly in a way that consumers do not delineate between the three. As Cook preaches, the company's core principle is that they only do a few things (meaning make a few products). And they'll only do things where they can make a significant contribution. Not financially, but a contribution to society at large. He says, "You know, we want to really enrich people's lives at the end of the day, not just make money. Making money might be a byproduct, but it's not our North Star."

Cook believes, additionally, that collaboration is essential for innovation. Religiously, every Monday at 9AM, Apple holds an executive team meeting. They spend 4 hours together and discuss everything "that's important." Cook claims that his top execs are the best in the world, and yet the secret to Apple's success is that they don't have that many people—that small teams do amazing things together. He also explains that his exec team has been there for a while, and have lived through different cycles. So they have a maturity, but they still have the boldness. They're still ready to burn the bridge. He says, "I mean no company would have done what we did this year. Think about it. We changed the vast majority of our iPhone in a day. We didn't kind of—you know, change a little bit here or there. iPad, we changed the entire lineup in a day. The most successful product in consumer electronics history, and we change it all in a day and go with an iPad mini and a fourth-generation iPad. Who else is doing this? Eighty percent of our revenues are from products that didn't exist 60 days ago. Is there any other company that could do that?

Maybe more companies should because, as Cook explains, "In fact, there are all these tablets that have come out last year as well—and the usage of them appears to be very low. Certainly the data I'm seeing suggests—and this is all third-party data—that over 90 percent of the web-browsing traffic from tablets are from iPad. You may have seen the data over the weekend from IBM that was Black Friday sales that showed the iPad was used in more e-commerce transactions than any other device. And that's more than all Android devices combined, tablets and smartphones. Since these statistics do not correlate with unit sales, it suggests to me that the iPad user experience is so far above the competition, that the iPad has become a part of their lives, instead of a product that they buy and place in a drawer."

This represents the Apple-consumer circle of life—the fact that Apple focuses on products that truly enrich their customer's lives, which helps them positively impact society at large. And, because Apple is effectively executing their vision of building the best products; their customer's lives are in fact being enriched. Through this cycle, Apple has created devoted, cult-like brand enthusiasts.

And yet, the only way this whole process actually works is because those same brand loyalists Apple has created externally, Apple has also created internally. Cook states that what bonds Apple employees is their love for the company. They all want Apple to do great things. They all subscribe to the same principles: they believe in the simple, not the complex, believe in collaboration, and view that Apple is here to make the best products in the world. "I love the company. A significant part of my life is Apple. Maybe some people would say it's all of my life. I would say it's a significant part. And you know, I feel both a love for it, and feel a responsibility. I think this company is a jewel. I think it's the most incredible company in the world, and so I want to throw all of myself into doing everything I can do to make sure that it achieves its highest, highest potential," states Cook.

Hearing a public company's CEO describe his company in such a way really makes you believe in Apple's vision. While reading and learning about Cook, it's easy to see why Jobs picked him as his successor. Apple is a company that has changed the world in more ways than one, it has held the position of the world's most valuable company, and continues to best its competitors—and even itself. Jobs paved the way, and created a company destined for greatness—while Cook's job has been to carry on Apple's legacy. Although, when you're that passionate about something, and love a company that much—it is no job at all. And the same higher calling that was apparent in Steve Jobs is the same that shines through Tim Cook. And verifiable or not, it is the same spirit that radiates through Apple—making it the crowning company it is.

Bloomberg BusinessWeek, December 2012, Tim Cook's Freshman Year. Josh Tyrangiel

INC. MAGAZINE'S DISRUPTION: WHAT TRENDS TO KEEP AN EYE ON (IN JANUARY 2013)

Inc. released a special report on "2013 (and Beyond) Game Changing Trends, Hot Markets and Daring Predictions." The article showcased "5 New Niches that are Heating Up Fast" as well as "5 Game Changing Trends."

The five niches represent opportunities derived from openings in different industries through primarily, the use of disruptive technologies. Online education, disruptive design, power sleep, personal health and manufacturing in the U.S. embodied the niches.

For many years now there has been incessant grumbling about the necessary change our education system needed, but without much action. As Amish Jani of Firstmark Capital says, education is at a major crossroads in terms of exorbitant cost and the lack of direct correlation to improved life outcomes. This inefficiency represents a niche opportunity for entrepreneurs to build businesses for and take advantage of companies like Coursera and Udacity—which offer free online schooling by top professors from elite universities—have become practical and viable solutions. A handful of these types of programs have sprouted up and been able to attract hundreds of thousands of enrollments, while also lure in millions in venture funding. Inc. expects this niche to rapidly expand.

Disruptive design—startups upending stagnant product categories through the power of design—is another fast moving market. Inc. gives the examples of the Nest Thermostat and the Plumen CFL light bulb. As Scot Herbst, of Herbst Produkt, a top product-design firm explains, "Disruptive products are king, and innovative designs will challenge the status quo in ways that previously wouldn't have been possible."

Another category developing through the convergence of mobile technology and data analytics, plus the desire to get a better night's sleep, are sleep focused applications. My Jawbone UP for instance, through its wristband and mobile technology, tracks a user's nightly sleep patterns. The trend seems to be one with a lot of growth potential.

Another niche unfolding due to the intersection of technology and health are wearable fitness-tracking devices. According to ABI research, sales of wearable fitness-tracking devices like Fitbit, are projected to hit 90 million units in 2017, and the market for sports and fitness apps will exceed $400 million in 2016. The market enables consumers to monitor and improve their overall health through diet, sleep and exercise via digital tools. The adoption rate of such technologies is increasing and will create ample opportunity for entrepreneurs.

Lastly, partly due to the American business community preferring to spur the economy by keeping manufacturing in the States versus overseas, with the cost of overseas manufacturing rising and new technologies like 3-D printing, the last niche is American manufacturing. Thanks also, in part to the Maker Movement—a DIY revolution—America has witnessed a resurgence of small manufacturing in the States. This new course seems to be one with long-term implications and tremendous value.

As the aforementioned five niches represent early stage emerging opportunities, the five game changing trends encompass larger, more "seemingly" sustainable business opportunities, with substantiated data and proven business concepts. The five trends are: plastic will be passé, there will be an app for every waking minute, ads will be articles and vice versa, customers will get in your face and social media will get bigger and smaller.

As Inc. explains, plastic will be passé, smartphones are quickly displacing credit cards the way plastic once toppled cash. With Google Wallet, Google set the ball in motion. Now, other players are jumping in like—AT&T, Verizon Wireless and T-Mobile who are all uniting to create a mobile wallet named "Isis." Not surprisingly, however, entrepreneurs are making the biggest dent in the space. In 2009, the Jack Dorsey's Square offered simplified credit card processing through a mobile device credit card reader. Merchants can swipe cards via smartphone or tablet app in place of traditional credit card terminals thanks to Square. Additionally, consumers can use Square's mobile app to make purchases, literally creating a swipe-free transaction. eMarketer reports that purchases made on mobile devices in the U.S. are projected to reach $31 billion by 2015 up from roughly $11.6 billion in 2012. Approximately, roughly 34 percent of people surveyed by IDC Financial Insights in 2012 reported making mobile purchases, up from just 19 percent in 2011. The bottom line is that the inefficient and archaic way of handling transactions and making payments is being cleverly reinvented.

There will be an app for every waking minute, thanks in part to the fact that nearly half of all Americans own a smartphone. Globally, mobile users are projected to surpass desktop users as soon as 2014. As Inc. says, consequently, the amount of time we spend on mobile devices is rapidly rising—currently (in January 2013) an average of 82 minutes a day, more than twice the amount of time spent in 2010. According to ComScore, minutes spent per month on apps more than doubled from March 2011 to March 2012. And as David Mattin, lead strategist of trendwatching.com, explains, consumers are accustomed to—even addicted to—always-on, anywhere, anytime connectivity, and the next 12 months will see them push their mobile lust to obsessive, occasionally nearly insane degrees. App building entrepreneurs and businesses will gladly take advantage of these mobile maniacs by helping them decide what to do, where to eat, what to buy, all through the benefits anytime, any day, anywhere mobile apps.

Ads will be articles, and vice versa—thanks in part that everyone knows how to block banner ads and pop-ups, while the world is spending more time online. These activities have created a new way of marketing—Content Marketing. Content being anything from blog posts, white papers, podcasts, videos, slide shows and webinars. Creating the content is only half of the equation, however, marketers then must figure out how to engage their audience. Which has led to the rise of native advertising—which is simply advertising that follows the format, style and voice of the platform it appears in, attempting to make the advertising look much more organic rather than an outside intrusion. It appears to be effective: on Facebook, for instance, the average click-through rate for "sponsored stories" (FB's form of native advertising), in the second quarter of 2012, was 53 percent greater than that of display ads, reports TBG Digital. This type of marketing levels the playing field for startups. The reason being that the content doesn't have to be expensive to be effective and a lot of times, larger companies can get so focused on quality that they won't do something bold, while smaller companies can let go of quality and focus on results, explains James Gross, President of a software advertising company in New York. The opportunity doesn't stop there, as a number of companies are focusing on the service side of native advertising. Companies like Contently and Percolate that focus on content creation, and Sharethorugh who supports the placement of advertising. Inc. predicts we'll be seeing a lot more of this type of marketing, which creates innovative ways for brands to connect and engage their target market.

An Inc. states that in today's networked, hyper-informed economy, customers will get in your face. What they mean is that customers are no longer just buyers, but are helping design and innovate products that haven't even been created and even investing directly into the seed funding stage. Kickstarter—one of the top crowdfunding platforms which allow potential customers and interested parties to fund the development of the proposed project—is a prime example. But crowdfunding is merely scratching the surface. Quirky, a New York City based company uses a different model—it uses its community of inventors to vote on products the company will then choose to manufacture. Then, through the sales of the items, it rewards influencers (who helped define the product) with royalties of those sales, which gives influencers incentive to promote the items themselves. The model has essentially eliminated the need for traditional marketing; the nature of marketing is convincing people they need something—you don't need to persuade someone if they need something if they've already told you they need it, says Ben Kaufman, Quirky's founder and CEO. The key to success will be the forward-thinking entrepreneur who can harness the power of the different roles customers represent.

Social media will get bigger, and smaller. There were 1.43 billion social network users in 2012, a 19.2 percent increase from 2011. To name the majors, Facebook, Twitter, Google+, LinkedIn, Instagram, Pinterest—so many social media sites, empowering users to build massive social networks, with new sites constantly popping up. But as Inc. explains, at the same, the sheer massiveness of Facebook and the other social media sites is creating opportunities for smaller-scale niche networks. Some examples are Path, a free personal-social-network that limits users to 150 people (the idea is based on research from Dunbar's number, which claims humans can only maintain about 150 deep relationships), and Nextdoor, which helps users connect with others in the same geographic area.

2013 is posed to be a good year with unemployment declining, the housing market returning to pre-recession levels and the economy slowing healing. The niches and trends included in the Inc. report seem promising and worth a closer look, but only the future will tell what opportunities will actually be sustainable.

Inc. Magazine, December 2012/January 2013, How & Where to Make Money in 2013 (and Beyond). Adam Bluestein

BIG DATA: WEB 3.0

Reid Hoffman says that Big Data is in fact Web 3.0. In 2011, VC funding totaled $2.47 billion in big data. In April 2011, Splunk—the first Big Data star to go public—surged to a $3 billion valuation on the NASDAQ, despite its $121 million revenue.

Big Data is the massive, endlessly growing stockpile of digital information, ranging from stock price quotes, to Foursquare check-ins, to movie theater time info—and everything in between. Every piece of information will be collected, indexed, housed, distributed and analyzed by a rapidly progressing niche of companies, which represents the Big Data business opportunity. According to IBM, 2.5 quintillion bytes of data are created daily (enough to equal more than 531 million DVDs), and 90 percent of all the world's digital information was produced over the last two years. By 2020, the annual data-generation rate will inflate 4,300 percent to 35 zettabytes of intelligence, projects Falls Church, Virginia-based Computer Sciences Corporation (which is 7.35 trillion DVDs). "Big data represents a transformation of the entire IT industry and a $300 to $500 billion wealth-creation opportunity for entrepreneurs," says Matt Ocko, co-management partner of San Francisco investment fund Data Collective. "It's as sound a bet for us today as investing in PC-related technologies in 1981 or in internet-enabling technologies in 1994."

To understand the opportunity, let's take the health care industry, for instance. According to a report done by the McKinsey Global Institute, the potential value of Big Data, if used creatively and effectively by the U.S. health care industry, would be worth more than $300 billion in that sector every year. At the moment, health care providers discard 90 percent of that information. Here's an example: studies show that 20 percent of patients revealed from American hospitals need to be readmitted within 30 days, an inefficiency that costs Medicare $17 billion per year. Eric Horvitz, a computer scientist (and physician) who works at Microsoft research built a program called the readmissions manager, which Microsoft sells at part of its health care IT offerings. The program analyzes hospital data to produce a readmissions forecast for each patient, and doctors can tailor follow-up appointments based on the forecast, which stands to slash substantial costs, and that is just one example, of one program, in one market niche that Big Data will transform.

As a tool, Big Data is finding its way into fashion, finance, advertising, law enforcement, customer service and pretty much every commercial transaction on the planet. As Baratunde Thurston comments, if the prevalence of chatter about "Big Data" is any indicator, data has evolved from something we collect with the vague promise of future value to something we analyze to retrieve that value. Big Data is a big deal, and proving to us that numbers don't lie.

Entrepreneur Magazine, December 2012, Collection Agencies: The Rise of Big Data. John Patrick Pullen

Fast Company Magazine, December 2012/January 2013, Data is the New Language. Baratunde Thurston

Fast Company Magazine, July/August 2012, Let 1 Trillion Data Bloom. Farhad Manjoo

TIM O' REILLY:
THE TECHNOLOGY SOOTHSAYER

Tim O'Reilly has built his career on knowing what's coming next. He has unquestionably been at the forefront of every major tech trend since the late 70's, has continued to see the future before anyone else, while leading the tech revolution forward. Here's what Steven Levy says of him: his ability to quickly identify nascent trends is unparalleled. It was O'Reilly who first figured out that programming was becoming a mass skill. It was O'Reilly who realized in 1993 that the internet browser would broadly transform civilization, spurring him to form one of the first web portals, the Global Network Navigator. O'Reilly who recognized that open source would be a liberating engine of innovation so he created books and conferences around that theme. O'Reilly who saw the rebirth of the web as a participatory medium and launched the influential Web 2.0 Conference dedicated to promoting and plumbing that notion. O'Reilly who identified hackers as canaries in the coal mine of emerging technology, and O'Reilly who made a point of tapping the minds of such people—allowing his company to grasp and share the import of advances like WiFi, Big Data and the Maker Movement earlier than almost anyone else.

In 1978, three years after obtaining his degree, O'Reilly cofounded O'Reilly & Associates, his media company which started off publishing easy-to-understand computer manuals and technical guides for hardware companies. In 1992, O'Reilly & Associates published and released Ed Krol's "The Whole Internet User's Guide & Catalog, which became the company's first million-copies-sold best seller and one of the first books to make the Internet popular. By 1993, O'Reilly foresaw the value in the Internet and through O'Reilly & Associates launched the first web portal and first site to be supported by banner ads called the Global Network Navigator. In an interview with Steven Levy, O'Reilly recalls, "I had no idea it [the Internet] would be as big as it became. I still remember in 1993 my partner Dale Dougherty originally wanted to do Global Network Navigator as a quarterly online magazine. And I remember saying to him, 'Dale, I think people will have the web browser open every day. We have to think about them accessing it every day.' I had no idea that it would be every minute."

His vision paid off, and in 1995 AOL acquired the platform for $11 million. In 1997, O'Reilly & Associates hosted the first of what evolved into a massive gathering of developer conferences. A year later, attendees coined the term 'open source,' which evolved into the industry renowned Open Source Summit.

In 2000, O'Reilly flexed his influence by writing an open letter protest to the enforcement of Amazon's "one click" utility patent. Thanks to the cogent O'Reilly, Amazon CEO, Jeff Bezos, later united with O'Reilly pushing for patent reform.

By 2005, O'Reilly was another step ahead of the curve, and helped his partner Dale Dougherty launch Make Magazine, which contributed to catapulting the DIY revolution forward. The same year, he spun off O'Reilly Alpha Tech Ventures—a seed stage investment fund—with investments that include Codecademy, Bitly and Foursquare. In 2009, O'Reilly joined the board of directors of Code for America, a nonprofit that places programmers into city government to cut through bloated bureaucratic crap, and does the impossible by helping the government to be more efficient.

O'Reilly explains that his key in business is to create more value than he captures. For instance, at his company, they accomplish this by marketing big ideas instead of their own products. He states, "If companies don't think systematically enough—if they try to capture too much of the value—eventually innovation moves somewhere else."

O'Reilly has had a long, fulfilling career. He claims, although he hasn't obtained vast wealth as others in the sector, he is completely satisfied with what he's accomplished and the choices he's made, and hopes that those who have hit big will use their fortunes for good. After reading and hearing about O'Reilly, one starts to understand that his calling in the tech sector is that of someone destined to support, and facilitate the expansion of the tech world as a whole. Which begets the question—is it O'Reilly who sees the future before anyone else, or is it O'Reilly who in fact, creates the future we all see?"

Wired Magazine, January 2013, The Seer. Steven Levy, Katie M. Palmer

ROBOTS: BREAKING OUR CHAINS

Here is a quick history lesson from Kevin Kelly of Wired: Imagine that 7 out of 10 working Americans got fired tomorrow. What would they do? Seems farcical, right? Well, that in slow motion is exactly what the industrial revolution did to the entire workforce of the early 19th century. A couple hundred years ago, about 70 percent of the American labor forces were farmers. Today, a mere 1 percent of those jobs have been eliminated and replaced with machines. And, although those old jobs are now obsolete, automation created hundreds of millions of new jobs in entirely new industries. Today, almost all of us are doing jobs that the 1800 farmer could never have dreamed of.

Putting it plainly, it is only a matter of time before robots replace the jobs we currently have. As Kelly explains, this upheaval is being led by a second wave of automation, one that is centered on artificial cognition, cheap sensors, machine learning, and distributed smarts. Kelly says this deep automation will touch all jobs—from manual labor to knowledge work, from blue to white-collared jobs alike. Here is a likely scenario: first, robots will continue their takeover of jobs they've already infiltrated—they will finish replacing assembly line workers in the manufacturing space, warehouse workers, farming, road work and industrial cleaning. Simultaneously, robots will continue their journey into the corporate world. Any information-centered position is target—from attorney, to doctor, analyst, to reporter, architect and even computer programmer: the robot revolution will be widespread and relentless. And get this, the revolution has already begun.

The reason we are at this epic turning point is simple: machines have evolved, and now learn how we learn, just way better. Take for instance, IBM's supercomputer Watson, who beat the champs of Jeopardy in 2011. Watson acquired his smarts not by being programmed, but by actually reading all of Wikipedia (in human language, not machine language). Watson has introduced the world to the dawn of a new era of computing. As IBM'ers claim, the first era of computers were tabulating machines, ones that added up figures, the second being the programmable types—the mainframe, desktop, PCs, smartphones—all of the computers we have today, and Watson represents this third era, a truly cognitive moment where real artificial intelligence is born. These new computers (robots) such as Watson do not ask us to communicate with them in their coded language; they speak ours. But even more significant, they can learn on their own, meaning they can evolve without constant human direction.

I know, thanks to Hollywood this inevitably leads to the violent picture of robots taking over the world through murder and plunder, dancing in our heads. But Kelly says the revolution is a good thing. To understand the benefit, we need to analyze our relationship with robots, which Wired broke down into four categories.

Let's start with category 1: Jobs humans can do but robots can do even better. Examples of these types of jobs are routine X-ray analysis, airplane autopilot, tax preparation. Robots have proven themselves in manufacturing, and are working across the intelligence and service industries.

Next is category 2: Jobs that humans can't do but robots can. For instance, without the precision and controlled-detail movements of machine automation, we would not have a single computer chip or, think about any type of machine manufacturing—like the creation of a single brass screw that a human would have trouble making unassisted, but machines can turn out thousands per hour without flaw. No human, dead or alive, can search all the web pages in the world and return your web query, which is exactly what robots do every time you search. In other words, we aren't giving "good jobs" to robots; the jobs robots are currently doing are supporting the growth of society and enriching our daily lives. They are jobs, we as a species, could not even do.

Onto category 3: Robot jobs that we can't even imagine yet. With each advancement of technology come new industries and the formation of new jobs. As Kelly says, this is the greatest genius of the robot takeover: with the assistance of robots and computerized intelligence, we already can do things we never imagined doing 150 years ago. He explains, "We can remove a tumor in our gut through our navel, make a talking-picture video of our wedding, drive a cart on Mars, print a pattern on fabric that a friend mailed to us through the air. We are doing, and are sometimes paid for doing, a million new activities that would have dazzled and shocked the farmers of 1850. These new accomplishments are not merely chores that were different before. Rather, they are dreams that are created chiefly by the capabilities of the machines that can do them. They are jobs the machines make up."

This brings us to category 4: Jobs that only humans can do—at first. Kelly claims the one thing humans can do that robots can't is to decide exactly what it is humans want to do. Our inventions spur our desires, making this a circular process. Industrialization freed up humans' time to focus on the things humans wanted to do for work—jobs like athletes, musicians, actors, authors, fashion designers and the like. With the aid of machines, we are able to take on these roles, until the point when robots can do these things as well. Then, we will be given the opportunity to dream up what we'll do next. And the cycle will continue, even when most of today's work will be done by bots, our work tomorrow will be to figure out new things for robots to do that will later become repetitive jobs for the robots, freeing us up again to figure out what we want to do next. Our human mission will be to keep creating jobs for bots—and that is a job that will never end.

We mustn't fear the robot takeover; it will empower us to think harder, work smarter, dream bigger and advance civilization in ways we can't even imagine fathomable. Kelly says, "This is not a race against the machines. If we race against them, we lose. This is a race with the machines."

It just makes sense. If we outsource the jobs that make us like robots, robots will give us the freedom to be more human.

Wired Magazine, January 2013, Better than Human. Kevin Kelly

QUIRKY: OUTSOURCING CROWDSOURCING SUCCESS

Ben Kaufman founded Quirky in 2009, at the ancient age of 22 years old. Quirky's foundation is built on one of the latest tech trends—crowdsourcing. The company attracts investors to generate ideas, and has the community vote on which ideas are best to physically produce. The community then tests the products, and purchases the goods they helped design, while receiving a royalty on each of the products they helped finalize that makes them personally vested in the sales of the products.

Quirky has proven out its business model, and made $20 million through sales in 2012 alone. It has drawn the attention of smart money, and in the late 2012 raised $68 million in venture funding from Andreesen & Horowitz and Kleiner Perkins Caulfield & Byers to put towards the company's grand retail strategy.

At the moment (February 2013) the community is in the 300,000's with 65 investors, all whom earn more than $20,000 a year from their product visions. Each product passes through three points—the product evaluation, engineering and pricing stages—during the Quirky process, where at any point the idea can get derailed. The value the company provides to retailers is a never-ending pipeline of products rooted in consumer research. Since 2011, Quirky has complemented its online sales by securing shelf space at top retailers like The Container Store, Bed Bath & Beyond and Target. Most consumer product firms can only offer a few dozen products per season, while Quirky's cup on the other hand, runneth over with proven products.

The current funds raised are earmarked to scale the business, and Quirky plans to create subcommunities that will focus on specific verticals. The goal is to go from producing two items per week, to about ten.

Four years later, after the demise of most startups preaching crowdsourced innovation, outspoken critics and outright doubt about the viability of the business—Quirky's skeptics have been hushed. And Quirky is on track to accomplish its grand vision, "The ultimate goal is to build the 21st-century P&G based on people who wouldn't otherwise have a voice," says Ben Kaufman. What a novel concept, actually building products consumers want. It's quite hilarious it took a 22-year old visionary to figure it out.

Fast Company Magazine, February 2013, Community Building. Cliff Kuang

TWITTER COFOUNDERS: ATTEMPTING TO REINVENT THE WORLD'S CONVERSATION, AGAIN

For more than 20 years, Charlie Rose has hosted PBS's late night interview hour, the Charlie Rose Show. In February, 2013, Fast Company published an interview Charlie Rose hosted with Biz Stone and Ev Williams, cofounders of Twitter. Seated at Rose's iconic table in his television studio, the trio collaborated over the meaning of conversation in an age of information overload.

Despite Twitter being the *de facto* platform for short-character (tweets are limited to 140 characters) dialogue, Biz Stone affirms the importance of long-form conversation. He says, "Without long-form, deeper-dive, more relevant conversation, I don't think social media would have anything to be social or media about."

Ev Williams reaffirms Stone's thought by stating, "In the best case, they are complementary. The long form gives you ideas that you want to engage with people on, and the opposite can happen as well. Conversations that start as little blips can catch someone's imagination and turn into something much deeper. In the worst case, people get obsessed with the shortform.

Williams explains, that the evolution of conversation online, looked at very broadly, has been that over the past dozen years or so, most of our efforts, as well as lots of other people's has been about lowering the barrier, getting more voices into the public discourse. It started with blogs a dozen years ago, and everybody could be a publisher, everybody could have a voice. The theory, which turned out to be true in many cases, was that if they had something worthwhile to say, they would eventually find the right audience. Twitter is sort of the epitome of that. It can't really get any easier than sending a text message and have that be a globally available piece of media. But that doesn't necessarily lead to quality conversation. So the question now is, how do we raise the quality of the discourse? It's not just about quantity anymore.

The Twitter cofounders' two new projects—Branch and Medium—look to solve the elusive question of quality over quantity. Branch for example allows people to host dinner-party-like conversations that allow pretty much anybody to watch, but limits who are actually invited to sit down at the table to speak. Medium, their second project, is more like blogging. The idea is that anyone can contribute, and the best ideas flow to the top, and they can react off of one another. What makes it unique from most of the web is that it's less focused on the right now, and more on thoughtful things that evolve over time that have a longer shelf life. It is a way to put an idea out there in the world, work on it, and get feedback.

The two claim that their ultimate goal is to, "shift the discourse and decisions of society so it's not just about attention, or popularity, or page views, or clicks." They explain they are emotionally invested in the idea of large-scale systems that allow people to express themselves, which is why they gravitate towards these types of businesses. It speaks very much to their world-positive view. That people are basically good; if you give them the right tools, they'll prove it to you everyday.

Fast Company Magazine, February 2013, Reinventing Conversation. Fast Company Staff Twitter's Biz Stone And Ev Williams And Charlie Rose: The Long And Short Of Creative Conversations, February 2013. Fast Company Staff

THE POWER OF CONVERSATION: TWO THAT SHOOK THE GLOBE

Innovation is the spark that fuels disruption, and disruption changes the world we see. Innovation sometimes starts with an idea, and that idea may turn into a dialogue. That dialogue sometimes then morphs into something more.

In February 2013, Fast Company published a segment showcasing the art of dialogue, and in that segment an article titled '10 Conversations That Changed Our World.' From that article I grabbed two that I felt were the most impactful—the birth of Silicon Valley and the birth of Facebook. Thanks to Fast Company, here's a look at those conversations:

Most of the modern technology that we hold dear today—from laptops to ATMs to iPhones probably wouldn't exist if in 1957, a group of eight young geniuses hadn't banded together and left their brilliant but maniacal boss, William Shockley, to form the first venture-backed startup. Dubbed "the Traitorous Eight" by Shockley, the colleagues, who included future, Intel cofounders Gordon Moore and Robert Noyce, would go on to, and build the first practical integrated circuit and the first wave of valley companies. One of eight, Jay Last, now 83, recalls how it happened!

"Shockley was a brilliant scientist but a terrible manager. He'd won the Nobel Prize for inventing the transistor and started trying to make an impossible device that didn't work. So he took it out on us. We complained to Arnold Beckman, who funded Shockley labs. At first he sided with us, but when he confronted Shockley, Beckman left us adrift. We knew we couldn't keep working there.

One evening we met at the house of Vic Grinich [another member of the Traitorous Eight] to talk about our next move. We were all down-hearted, sitting in this dark-paneled room. We could get jobs easily, but we liked working together. That night, we made the decision to find some way that we could work as a group. But we were asking, how can we get a company to hire a group of eight people?

We sent a letter to Hayden, Stone & Co., a firm that the father of Eugene Kleiner [another member of the group] knew, telling them what we had to offer. Art Rock was a young guy working there, and he had the wit not to throw our letter in the wastebasket. He and his boss,

Bud Coyle, flew out to meet us and told us about this novel idea that was really the start of venture capital. Art said. 'The way you do this is you start your own company.' We were blown away. There was no concept of funding a group back then. Hayden, Stone & Co. agreed to find us a backer.

After being turned down by 30 people, we met with Sherman Fairchild, whose father was one of the first IBM investors. He invested $1.5 million in our group to create Fairchild Semiconductor. The eight of us, plus Hayden, Stone, owned the company, and we had a buyout option after a five-year period.

We didn't realize at the time the legacy we'd leave. If you trace the family tree, several hundred companies came out of Fairchild. I helped start Silicon Valley. Thank God Shockley was so paranoid or we'd still be sitting there."

'In 2003, Harvard sophomore Mark Zuckerberg took on a project for the now famous Winklevoss twins while also developing "The Facebook." An instant-messaging conversation with Adam D'Angelo, a high school friend, helped clarify his priorities.'

Zuck:	So you know how I'm making that dating site
Zuck:	I wonder how similar that is to the facebook thing
Zuck:	Because they're probably going to be released around the same time
Zuck:	Unless I fuck the dating site people over and quit on them right before I told them I'd have it done.
D'Angelo:	haha
Zuck:	Like I don't think people would sign up for the facebook thing if they knew it was for dating
Zuck:	and I think people are skeptical about joining dating things too.
Zuck:	But the guy doing the dating thing is going to promote it pretty well.
Zuck:	I wonder what the ideal solution is.
Zuck:	I think the facebook thing by itself would draw many people, unless it were released at the same time as the dating thing.
Zuck:	In which case both things would cancel each other out and nothing would win. Any ideas? Like is there a good way to consolidate the two.
D'Angelo:	We could make it into a whole network like a friendster. haha. Stanford has something like that internally
Zuck:	Well I was thinking of doing that for the facebook. The only thing that's different about theirs is that you like request dates with people or connections with the facebook you don't do that via the system.
D'Angelo:	Yeah

Zuck: I also hate the fact that I'm doing it for other people haha. Like I hate working under other people. I feel like the right thing to do is finish the facebook and wait until the last day before I'm supposed to have their thing ready and then be like "look yours isn't as good as this so if you want to join mine you can . . . otherwise I can help you with yours later." Or do you think that's too dick?

D'Angelo: I think you should just ditch them

And the rest is history.

Fast Company Magazine, February 2013, 10 Conversations That Changed Our World. Jillian Goodman, J.J. McCorvey, Margaret Rhodes, and Linda Tischler

DUNBAR'S NUMBER:
THE "SOCIAL FIBONACCI SEQUENCE"

A little more than 10 years ago, Oxford University Professor Robin Dunbar substantiated an interesting societal secret, while studying Christmas-card-sending habits of the English. This was pre-social media, and Dunbar wanted to determine a benchmark for meaningful social connections. Not how many people the average person knew, per se, but the number of deep relationships. He decided the best way to find those connections was to follow holiday cards. After all, sending holiday cards is an investment of time, energy and mental focus and most people won't incur them for just anybody.

Dunbar teamed up with anthropologist Russell Hill, and mapped out the average English household's holiday card network. Their research showed that roughly a quarter of cards went to family, about two-thirds to friends, and 8 percent to colleagues. Most important to their findings, however, was a single number: the total number of cards sent out per household. That number was 153.5, or approximately 150.

150 was the exact number Dunbar expected. Over the past twenty years, researchers have found groups of roughly 150 everywhere they looked. As Drake Bennett of Bloomberg BusinessWeek explains, anthropologists studying the world's remaining hunter-gatherer societies have found that clans tend to have 150 members; throughout western military history, the size of the company—the smallest autonomous military unit—has hovered around 150; the self-governing communes of the Hutterites, an Anabaptist sect similar to the Amish and the Mennonites, always split when they grow larger than 150; so do the officers of W. L. Gore & Associates, the materials firm famous for innovative products such as Gore-Tex and for its radically nonhierarchical management structure that when a branch exceeds 150 employees, the company breaks it in two and builds a new office.

There are outliers in either direction, but in general, the research has found that once a group grows larger than 150, members lose their feeling of connection. Dunbar writes, "The figure of 150 seems to represent the maximum number of individuals with whom we can have a genuinely social relationship, the kind of relationship that goes with knowing who they are and how they relate to us. Putting it another way, it's the number of people you would not feel embarrassed about joining uninvited for a drink if you happened to bump into them in a bar."

Bennett writes, as group size grows, a dizzying amount of data must be processed. A group of five has a total of 10 bilateral relationships between its members; a group of 20 has 190; a group of 50 has 1,225. Such a social life requires a big neo cortex, the layers of neurons on the surface of the brain, where conscious thought takes place. In his 1992 paper, Dunbar plotted the size of the neo cortex of each type of primate against the size of the group it lived in: the bigger the neo cortex, the larger the group a primate could handle. At the same time, even the smartest primate—us—doesn't have the processing power to live in an infinitely large group. To come up with a predicted human group size, Dunbar plugged our neo cortex ratio into his graph and got 147.8. This was the arithmetic that led to his argument—bigger brains equal bigger groups, which have cemented his role in the industry as the father of what's known as the "Social Brain Hypothesis."

Dunbar's collaboration has encompassed a myriad of disciplines—from physicists, to linguists, economists, anthropologists, archaeologists, and computer scientists—with an emphasis on the Social Brain Hypothesis. Dunbar has contributed to the New Scientist Magazine, Scotsman Newspaper, has given talks at TED and written books for the mainstream. Recently, his influence has resonated with a new crowd—startup entrepreneurs who build social media sites. Bennett says, at Facebook and at startups such as Asana and Path, Dunbar's ideas are regularly invoked in the attempt to replicate and enhance the social dynamics of the face-to-face world.

Case in point, Path, one of the latest social media sites, founded by Dave Morin, Shawn Fanning of Napster and Sean Parker of Napster and Facebook, is built solely on whatever has become known as "Dunbar's Number." The site, built in 2010, limits its users to 150 friends. The service has recently passed 5 million members, and Morin says keeping its network size small has rewarded the company with a remarkably engaged user base. He says the site is in the midst of launching several features that stem from the scientist's ideas, and the search algorithm Path uses to find a member's closest friends is derived directly from Dunbar's research. "What Dunbar's research represents is that no matter how the march of technology goes on, fundamentally we're all human, and being human has limits," says Morin.

As with all great research, there are those that critique, criticize and charge Dunbar with oversimplifying the depth of human interactions. Regardless, Dunbar continues to find his number surfacing everywhere—research published in 2011 found that on Twitter, the average number of other users a single user interacts with regularly falls between 100 and 200, and although the limit of friends a user can have on Facebook is a whopping 5,000, the average user has 190 (which falls in line with what Dunbar claims is the margin of error). Bennett writes that the venture capitalist Jerry Murdock, one of Path's investors and investor to Twitter and Tumblr, sees Dunbar's number as a sort of social Fibonacci sequence, a simple mathematical relationship revealing a deeper truth about the workings of the Universe. As Dunbar himself explains the number in a technology context, "The question is, 'Does digital technology in general allow you to retain the old friends as well as the new ones and therefore increase the size of your social circle?' The answer seems to be a resounding no, at least for the moment."

And as Bennett writes, "Language," as Dunbar explains, "is how humans used their big brains to get to 150. And, until something as revolutionary as that comes along, 150 is where we will stay."

Bloomberg BusinessWeek, January 2013, The Dunbar Number. Drake Bennett

GOOGLE'S LARRY PAGE: CHANGING THE WORLD 10X OVER

"If you're not doing something crazy, you're doing the wrong things," claims Google CEO Larry Page. Page lives life by the doctrine of 10x. Here's why, as Page says, a ten percent improvement means that you're basically doing the same thing as everybody else; you probably won't fail spectacularly, but you are guaranteed not to succeed wildly. Page's leadership style is a breath of fresh air, to an otherwise stuffy climate. And thanks to Page, as Steven Levy puts it, Google, despite some missteps and scrutiny from regulators, remains a flagship for optimists who believe that innovation will provide us with not just delightful gadgetry but solutions to our problems and inspiration for our dreams.

It is Page's 10x gospel that has powered Google to develop its skunk-works team; a team that identifies and executes seemingly impossible, technology-based projects. Google X, as it's come to be known, is behind such projects as Google's self-driving car, and Google Glass—the eye-wear computing system.

It was an undergrad, at the University of Michigan—while enrolled in a student leadership training program called Leadershape, which pushes its members to reach for the impossible— that Page found his 10x calling, and hasn't looked back since he graduated in 1995 with a degree in Engineering, and a year later in what he describes as a "vivid dream," started building a search engine he dubbed "BackRub." By 1998, Larry Page and Sergey Bin, formally launched Google—which it came to be called—from a friend's house, while maxing out three credit cards to purchase the initial hardware.

Six short years after launching Google, Page broke the Wall Street status quo by running Google's IPO as a rarely seen modified Dutch auction, making it easier for the general public to get in on the action.

2006 led to Page investing in a little unknown electric car company called Tesla, satisfying his long-standing 10x-desire, which was to build electric cars.

After serving as Google's President of products for ten years, Page took the CEO reigns from Eric Schmidt, in 2011. In a rare interview with Page as CEO, he spoke to Wired about his 10x creed, and how Google facilitates innovation. He says, "It's not easy coming up with 'moon shots.' And we're not teaching people how to identify those difficult projects. Where would I go to school to learn what kind of technological programs I should work on? You'd probably need a broad technical education and some knowledge about organization and entrepreneurship. There's no degree for that. Our system trains people in specialized ways, but not to pick the right projects to make a broad technological impact."

He explains that he has had grand visions to execute personal "moon shots," like his driverless car and Google Glasses for decades but admits the only thing that changed since then, are the guts to actually do it.

Yet, since Google's creation, Page has made 10x a foundational pillar, in which it executes business strategies. Steven Levy provides some instances. For example, Gmail provides 100 times more storage than its competitors, Google Translate provides translations from and to any language across the web, Google Books give access to nearly every book ever created, and as of recently (in an effort to test the experiment's efficacy), Google laid fiber optic cable across Kansas City to empower customers with broadband at 100 times industry-standard speeds.

2012, two years after Google X was formed, the secret lab introduced to the world its latest 10x invention. Google Glass is a wearable computer, with the sole mission to advance "hands-free" devices. The device itself projects information onto a lens above the user's right eye, enabling the user a very 10x experience. Name another company putting the World Wide Web into seeing glasses?

The same year, Page launched the "Solve for X Event," where 46 entrepreneurs, innovators and scientists gather to spit-ball 10x technology ideas. 2012 also marked the year that Page established the Global Impact Awards, which is an award for nonprofits that use technology to solve the world's toughest human challenges; such projects like Real-time clean water sensors and DNA barcoding.

Page's 10x philosophy has not only been the root of his wild personal success, but has carried over into Google's which has literally transformed the world we know—YouTube has forever enhanced the way we interact with and create online content, Google+ gave us an alternative to Facebook, Apple proved to the world how hard Google worked to map the entire globe. With its Google Maps, Android has taken the smartphone industry by storm, while providing an open source operating system for developers to build from, even with its core business Search, Google organized the entire web and empowered world-wide adoption. Google X will change the way the world drives, and how we compute. The team has even come up with an artificial brain, in which a cluster of computers running advanced algorithms learn from the world around them, much like humans do—helping spawn the beginning of a new era in computing. And this all stems from one man's simple mantra: think bigger, don't settle for a mere 10 percent increase, but push for 10 times. This mentality has single-handedly pushed civilization forward, set an astronomical benchmark for other companies to follow and advanced technology in ways the rest of us thought were just crazy how 10x of him?

Wired Magazine, February 2013, Think Bigger, Big Thinker. Steven Levy, Victoria Tang

KEVIN ROSE:
THE TECH VISIONARY NEXT DOOR

In 2004, with a couple thousand bucks and a basic level of programming, Kevin Rose unleashed Digg.com. Digg is a crowdsourced news site that allows anyone to vote on which articles are the most important. The site established him as champion to the Web 2.0 Movement, which paved the way for Facebook, Twitter, Path, and pretty much every online media startup in existence. With the launch of Digg, Rose Acquired instant rock-star like fame. He embraced the role while creating and starring in his weekly online video show called "Diggnation," which was basically him chugging beer, talking about the hottest Digg stories and just geekin' out. The show attracted 250,000 viewers a week, and as Max Chafkin of Fast Company puts it, "Venture capitalists showered Rose with cash, Rupert Murdoch and Barry Diller tried to buy his company, and BusinessWeek put Rose's baby-faced beheadphoned visage on the cover with the headline 'How This Kid Made $60 million in 18 Months,' even though that then gaudy number represented the most optimistic interpretation of his unrealized paper worth."

For aspiring and fellow tech entrepreneurs (like myself), Rose represented a whole new class of entrepreneur. Unlike Gates or Zuckerberg—Ivy-League-dropout-prodigies, Rose was a guy next door non-genius (Rose struggled in school, didn't focus, couldn't read well, and was somewhat lost in his late teens and early twenties). Despite his shortcomings, his vision still shook the world. As Chafkin affirms, Rose made the idea of being a founder accessible and fun. Some of his fans, including Pinterest CEO Ben Silbermann, were inspired to start companies of their own.

While building Digg and enjoying celebrity-like stardom, Rose stayed on his grind. In 2007, he made his first angel investment of $25,000 into OMGPOP, purchased shares of Twitter in 2008, and made a handful of investment plays in 2009. Simultaneously to growing Digg, luxuriating in the limelight and taking on his newfound angel investor role, Rose built another side project—an internet TV network called "Revision3," which he used to produce Diggnation. Revision3 would later be purchased by Discovery Communications for a cool $30 million, in May 2012.

As Chafkin explains, "By the time Rose's investors finally sold Digg in July 2012, to New York-based Betaworks for a price reported to be just $500,000, Rose was long gone. He formally left the social news site in March 2011 and almost immediately founded an app incubator, called Milk, as an attempt to reconcile his ADD nature with the demands of a Silicon Valley startup. The idea, backed by many of Rose's good friends, was a lab full of app developers who would produce a handful of projects a year. Rose says, that he liked the idea of being very up-front with his investors about the fact that they didn't have that one big idea that they were going after."

Even focusing on multiple projects through Milk couldn't satisfy his ADD nature, however. And, in May 2012 Google acquired the seven-person team for an amount between $15 million and $30 million.

The acquisition led Rose to follow his investor calling, and weeks after the Google offer, Rose joined Google Ventures—Google's seed stage $300 million-a-year venture arm. Rose runs it down like this, "I focus on consumer internet. Sometimes it's a working prototype; sometimes it's an idea on a napkin. I don't do a ton of deals a year, and I really like working with startups—it's the only way I can invest. It fits my ADD brain."

Unlike his Google counterparts who operate out of the firm's Mountain View offices, Rose enjoys the freedom to work at his home office and San Francisco cafés. He does not need to seek approval to make investments and anything up to $250,000 is easy. "A couple of coffees, a couple of e-mails and a handshake to seal the deal," Rose explains. "My big selling point is that I can drive a lot of early adoption. So what they get is someone who is pretty well connected to the industry and someone who is well connected to the product."

Rose invests up to $250,000 in his Google venture deals, opposed to up to $50,000 when he was flying solo, and as his investments grow, he will have the chance to lead larger, later-stage VC rounds. And, he says that if he ever launches a new company he will be able to use Google's war chest of resources to get it launched. Three hours a day Rose scrubs the web seeking new products, ideas and companies, while the rest of his time is dedicated to meeting with entrepreneurs.

The proliferation of super-angels—such as Ron Conway—has made the seed stage investment niche fiercely competitive. Chafkin says, Rose stands out by his charisma, his network, and the fact that the entrepreneur pitching him may very well have grown up wanting to be like Kevin Rose.

Rose claims that he wants to be one of the most accurate investors that ever lived. "In five years, I want people to look at my portfolio and say, 'Holy shit, he's a good picker.'"

"Kevin has always had a very good sense of what is cool on the Internet. People who are less geeky than him can't get beyond the surface of a product. And people who are more geeky than him tend to get mesmerized by the technology without seeing whether it's something that normal people can use," says Daniel Burka, Digg's former design director and Kevin's friend.

Of the 11 investments Rose has made, he's earned a return of about 22x his initial investment (and still hasn't liquidated his stakes in Fab, which is currently valued at $600 million, and Square valued at $3.25 billion) that will increase his returns.

Rose's track record has been somewhat flawless, with investments in pretty much every significant web darling in the past five years—Facebook, Twitter, Fab, Square, Path and Zynga. Some of his most impressive yields have come from lesser known startups—Chomp, for instance was acquired by Apple for $50 million, OMGPOP that Zynga bought for $200 million and ngmoco, which has sold to a Japanese gaming company at $400 million—which he had an uncanny eye to spot.

Rose, 35, has had an already impressive run—he changed the world with his creative vision, and has been flawlessly able to spot others with the same world-changing abilities. He has made a fortune investing, and Google believes so much in his talents, that they were willing to pay a handsome dowry to get him on the team. And, even after all his success, Rose is still the beer-loving guy next-door, everyone wants to be—maybe now, even more so than before.

Fast Company Magazine, February 2013, The Zen Master of Silicon Valley Chatter. Max Chafkin

GITHUB:
SUPPLYING SOFTWARE ITS TEETH

Sometimes technology happens by accident—for instance, the investors of the Post-it note were actually looking to develop a super-adhesive. Another illustration, what started as a nerdy endeavor with zero mainstream motive, has since arose as the most omnipotent software development tool on the planet.

In a few short years, GitHub has become the epicenter for all software developers, across the world, to easily share code and collaborate. GitHubs's momentum has been astounding: the company says it took 38 months to host its millionth project on the site; the five millionth came in just two months and 21 days. This phenomenal fact is one of the reasons that renowned Silicon Valley venture fund Andreesen Horowitz made its biggest investment to date, coinvesting with the Godfather of Silicon Valley—Ron Conway; into a GitHub venture round worth $100 million, valuing the five year old startup at $750 million.

Preston-Werner and Chris Wanstrath created GitHub in an effort to solve what Preston-Werner refers to as a "pain-in-the-ass problem." By using a version control system called "Git" developed by Linus Torvalds (the creator of Linux), the two set out to simplify collaboration amongst developers. A version control system is a tool that allows multiple coders to work on the same piece of code without losing track of the various changes made in each version or allowing the source code to be corrupted with lots of contradictory fixes. Torvalds built Git in reaction to the centralized structure of previous version control tools, which made it all but impossible for developers to work together independently. And despite the fact that Torvalds' system "makes collaboration possible, it doesn't make it easy," says Preston-Werner. He knew that Git could be this super powerful thing if only you could understand it."

And so, in October 2007, the two took it upon themselves to upgrade Git partly to make it more effective for their professional lives, but more importantly for fun. They both stayed at their day jobs and tinkered on the project at night. They took on two additional cofounders to support the mission, PJ Hyett and Scott Chacon, and by February 2008, GitHub was live.

Unlike many of its Web 2.0 counterparts, GitHub has an effective business model. Simply, GitHub provides companies and programmers a choice: they can use the collaborative platform for free as a place to build open-source software, or pay to use it as closed-source software, where they can program proprietary code that creates part of a commercial product. In the first instance, your goodwill to make your code available to everyone awards you the opportunity to take advantage of the army of open-source coders working on the GitHub platform. In the second, your company's programmers work in confidential, utilizing the collaborative tools GitHub has created but not its dispersed global force of talent. In the same breath, GitHub is like a junkyard and assembly line. Programmers on the platform can go pick out, or help develop, pretty much all of the open-source raw materials they need to build their product and set up their own closed work space to integrate those materials with their existing products.

In a March 2013 Inc. article, Will Bourne gives an example about GitHub, of the power in the site: today, a programmer in Dubai can drop a chunk of code in a "repository" on GitHub's site, post a description of his project and what kind of help he's looking for, and then watch as coders around the world dig in and contribute. If the software is open-source (that is, free for the taking by anyone who wants it, with minimal restrictions), the "repo" is visible to all three million developers who work on github.com. Depending on how interesting the idea is—it might be a simpler feature for a website or an entire operating system—hundreds or even thousands of people might "fork" or copy, the code and start working to improve it. When a developer thinks he has cracked whatever problem or portion of the problem he was working on, he can make a "pull request" to the "maintainer" of the repository to review his suggested fixes. The maintainer integrates some or all of the new code as he sees fit.

It was more than just the 300 percent year-over-year annualized growth—equating to 10,000 new users a day—that piqued Andreesen Horowitz' interest. GitHub, some of whose customers pay more than $1 million a year, has made money almost from its founding, up to that point without a cent of outside funding and without building any sort of formal sales organization being that the founding team members are all engineers.

GitHub has three payment options. The first is a personal plan that costs as low as $7 a month (the price is dependent on how many repositories you have). The second is an organization plan that has more advanced features for more sophisticated team management and starts at $25 per month. The last is the big-money enterprise option, which involves clients downloading a version of GitHub to live locally on their servers, and can cost millions of dollars a year. Enterprise clients encompass big names from Microsoft to Walmart, Lockheed Martin and LivingSocial. The company has hundreds of thousands of paying customers between the website and enterprise client base. A single project on GitHub's platform can represent months or even years of work and endless strings of dialogue between maintainers and coders contributing to the project. Which is exactly the point, open source on GitHub means that a startup doesn't have to begin from scratch; the team can pick out prefab pieces of foundational code, writing only the parts it needs to launch its product.

"The network effect is awesome. GitHub represents a new killer app for the Internet—a 'mini-web,' as Preston-Werner describes it.

As Bourne explains, "that "network effect" gets reinforced in numerous ways." For example, a developer on GitHub acquires a social reputation, and that reputation becomes a way to find new, paying work; that network's role as a placement service helps it grow still larger. "The truly badass potential of GitHub, though, is that it isn't only a force multiplier for producing code but also for the generation of ideas—and for the products created from those ideas," states Bourne.

Which is why Preston-Werner says, "Projects hosted on GitHub will increasingly be not just code but anything that involves working on files from a computer: books, hardware, projects, schematics for circuit boards, legal documents—anything that ends up in a digital format." It is already happening on the site with books, hardware and government.

Wanstrath says, "We want to enable people who don't know each other to collaborate on the same thing toward the same goal. This is all I want to do—forever."

GitHub has successfully been able to harness the human desire to contribute to a shared goal, and empowered people to look at the world collaboratively. David ten Have, founder and CEO of Ponoko (a company focused on developing 'the tools to enable digital fabrication') states, "GitHub is important beyond software: ethos and attitude are transferable—into lawmaking, product design, manufacturing, biology, chemistry, dance, music, moviemaking, books, cooking . . . the list goes on."

Marc Andreesen says software is eating the world, and it's been said that 'GitHub is where much of that software gets its teeth.'

Inc. Magazine, March 2013, It's GitHub's World. Will Bourne

BUSINESS STRATEGY:
THE FUTURE OF INCUBATORS

As if the incubator space wasn't crowded enough, here come the big boys. Large corporations are looking to leverage entrepreneurial innovation and cunning, by establishing incubators or funds aimed at startups. Companies such as Nike, Microsoft, PepsiCo, Johnson & Johnson and even American Express have each partnered with prominent or created incubators, early stage investment funds and other programs geared towards upstarts.

For startups, the opportunity represents a chance to receive investment, while getting real-time feedback about their product and the potential to land a major client in the process. Most of the programs are simply ran through an online open application process, with links typically found on the corporation's website.

For corporations, these endeavors portray an opportunity to find new ideas early on and conceivably partner with, invest in, or learn from today's most innovative entrepreneurs. For instance, Nike partnered with Techstars to create a 3-month mentorship program, for entrepreneurs building technologies for Nike's activity-tracking devices (like its FuelBand), each who receive a $20,000 investment and the ability to pitch investors and Nike at the end of the program. So did Microsoft who teamed up with Techstars to bring a 3-month incubator to Seattle for all startups designing products for Microsoft, Kinect and Windows Azure. PepsiCo created a digital incubator that selects startups in entertainment, mobile, retail and sustainability to receive funding paired with PepsiCo brands, like Frito-Lay or Gatorade, for mentoring and pilot campaigns. Johnson & Johnson has created a handful of innovation centers, scattered across the globe to fund early-stage life science companies.

These programs illustrate a paradigm shift in how startups engage and interact with large corporations. Fundamentally, it takes the guesswork out of what corporations want, unlocks a new avenue of early stage capital and enables all parties to waste less of each other's time and energy.

Inc. Magazine, April 2013, Strategy—Friends in High Places. Jennifer Alsever

CAPITAL STRATEGY: THE FUNDING GAP OF THE "SERIES A CRUNCH"

There is an ugly rumor named the "Series A Crunch," that has been circling the startup skies, looking for a place to land. The rumor—that venture capitalists are not funding startups, specifically in the typical series "A round" of investments, marked at $1 million or more—is complex indeed.

To clear the air a bit, the rumor isn't exactly true. First, venture industry deals as a whole, especially in the first rounds of VC funding (the Series A), has become increasingly fierce. Pair that with a small decrease of venture funding in 2012—according to a report released by the National Venture Capital Association, VC firms invested 10 percent less capital in private companies in 2012 than 2011—and it's easy to start to see why entrepreneurs are feeling a cash crunch.

That's only one side of the equation though. More notably perhaps, is the fact that the number of Series A investments (typically more than $1 million) hasn't kept up with the recent surge in the number of angel and seed investments (deals usually ranging from $25,000 to several hundred thousands). According to PitchBook, an investment research company, the number of Series A investments from 2008 to 2012 (118 to 244), has steadily increased and even doubled. Yet, seed-stage deals exploded roughly 262 percent, from 225 deals done in 2008 to 814 in 2012. Which is what Katherine Barr, General Partner at Mohr Davidow Ventures in Menlo Park, CA explains, "The real issue surrounding the Series A crunch is not that there are fewer Series A investments, it's just that a ton of companies have received seed funding in recent years. It's simply an issue of supply and demand."

With the increase of early stage funding, more startups are getting off the ground, but not necessarily receiving the follow-on funding. Entrepreneurs are starting to see that raising seed funding does not guarantee Series A investment down the road. Some 1,000 recently seed funded companies are projected to be "orphaned," unable to close later stage investment, claims CB Insights, a research team in New York City. Tyler Newton, a partner of catalyst investors in New York, says, "That's the nature of VC funding. Not every company that gets seed funding deserves to get Series A, and not every company that gets Series A deserves Series B. I believe there is still more venture money available than good deals to be made."

Whether Newton's belief is true or not, this landscape represents an opportune time and strong case for the lean startup. Rather than assuming your idea is worth pursuing, get your product out into the market, test the assumption and measure potential customer behavior. If you're correct, and built a product people actually want, no matter what the investment climate looks like at the time, investors will have interest. Or, you could follow the pack, raise a bunch of money, build your product, and waste everyone's time and energy realizing there is zero demand and zero follow-on capital. The choice is yours.

Inc. Magazine, April 2013, Where Has All the Funding Gone? Darren Dahl

INC. MAGAZINE'S TOP INDUSTRY PICKS: A LOOK FORWARD

To conclude my writing and research, what better than to finish with showcasing a handful of industries that are heating up and have potential staying power? In April, 2013, Inc. published an article titled 'The Eight Best Industries for Starting a Business.' Not all were relevant to the tech space, so I pulled four that I felt illustrated ample opportunity.

The first industry has potential to be as huge as the smartphone market. Wearable computing, as it is referred to, has already established its presence in the sports world and is looking to breakout into all areas of life. Google (with its Google X Glass project) and Microsoft are both innovating wearable computing in the glasses department while Kickstarter's Pebble (a startup that raised $30 million in ten days on the site) and Apple are focused on "smart watches." In the future we can expect to see clothing and even contact lenses that provide computing power that will shape our environment, giving us real-time feedback about our surroundings and explaining what we can do with the information. Another way to think about this segment is "augmented reality," which are computer-generated objects that appear within the real world, ultimately leading us to a better state of ubiquitous computing. Ubiquitous computing devices eventually disappear into the background simply leaving us with the core benefit of computing—the information and what we can do with it in real-time. Juniper Research reports the industry is already an $800 million industry and projects it will double in the next year. In terms of barriers to industry growth, the technology itself may prove to be a hindrance, at least initially. "Always-on" connections have to be managed and dependability can still be problematic. Battery life can be short, and ultimately, consumers have to understand the true value of the devices.

The next space that has captured the attention of aspiring entrepreneurs, VCs and anyone seeking higher education fed up with the status quo is online education. With college tuition costs steadily increasing, the job market remaining flat, driving more people to seek higher education to differentiate their value in the workplace, making the space even more crowded, the time is ripe for the disruption of traditional education. In the past year, the space has witnessed a wave of startups providing free online education many boasting of top professors from top universities. Kaplan and Apollo Group, parent of the University of Phoenix, and top universities such as Harvard, Stanford and MIT are all developing online courses. However, startups including 2U, Coursera and the Minerva Project are making the most waves, attracting millions from prominent venture capitalists and up to hundreds of thousands in class enrollees. According to research firm MarketsandMarkets, the content segment of online education could hit $72.9 billion by 2017.

Tim O'Reilly explains that the DIY Maker Movement is not just about individuals taking back their right to get their hands dirty and build the products they envision, but just as important are the new possibilities hardware is bringing to the world. Nothing encompasses the latter point than the sector's latest hardware innovation—3-D printers. 3-D printing is quickly taking the world by storm with industry analysts' worldwide projecting the market could reach $3 billion by 2018. Depending on your size and power of your printer, with commercial printers ranging from $20,000 to $600,000 and personal 3-D printers costing about $500, you can create anything from prosthetics to aerospace parts, or product prototypes to simply designed toys and jewelry. The moment has come where if you can dream it, you can print it.

The final industry on the list is providing companies the ability to be safe and sound in the cloud. In 2012 alone, virtual data rooms hit $600 million, and according to research from IBISWorld, that number is expected to explode to $1.2 trillion by 2017. Virtual data rooms allow users to store and access vast amounts of documents in the cloud, like Dropbox on steroids. Many provide tracking services and empower users to permit who is allowed to view what documents. Customers are those with complex transactions in which massive amounts of information change hands (like financial deals and lawsuits), where those transactions are highly sensitive and complicated. There has been a ton of action in the space as of late, with the big dogs—Merrill and RR Donnelly—providing proprietary services, and private equity and VC firms placing bets. Yet, with the projected dollar amount of the industry, there remains endless opportunity.

In the tech world, what is dominant today is not even relevant tomorrow—it's important to study the sector, understand the competition and follow your gut—choose wisely when targeting a sector.

Inc. Magazine, April 2013, The Eight Best Industries for Starting a Business. April Joyner, Judith Ohikuare, Jeremy Quittner, Julie Strickland, Samuel Wagreich

IN CLOSING

I've always been in love with tech, but it wasn't until I was about 22 years old that I saw it as more than just a hobby. Since then, my passion has turned into an almost maniacal obsession. Tech has become the fuel for my drive, the substance of my dreams and the reason for my existence. Alright, maybe that is a little dramatic, but I truly feel I was placed in this world to do business, and succeed in the tech sector by positively impacting the world. And I know there are many others that feel the same way. My writing is a tribute to them. To those of us still embarking on our journey, enjoying the ride towards many of the final destinations we will savor, while maintaining an unstoppable fortitude no matter how grim the circumstance.

I hope my writing shines light on what it takes to accomplish your dreams, gives in-depth insight into the nooks and crannies of the tech space and spurs your imagination to dream bigger and push farther than your natural limits could ever allow. Or, at the very least, I hope you have some cool new coffee table decor.

The world belongs to the endlessly curious, to those of us who see it eyes wide open, and never stop exploring.

Cheers!

Andrew Medal

April, 2013